American Literature in Context after 1929

Literature in Context

Literature in Context is an important new series that provides readers with relevant historical knowledge that deepens their understanding of American and British literature. Each accessible volume discusses the issues and events that engaged writers and provides original and useful readings of important literary works that demonstrate how context contributes to meaning.

American Literature in Context to 1865
Susan Castillo

American Literature in Context from 1865 to 1929
Philip R. Yannella

American Literature in Context after 1929
Philip R. Yannella

American Literature in Context *after 1929*

Philip R. Yannella

WILEY-BLACKWELL

A John Wiley & Sons, Ltd., Publication

This edition first published 2011

© 2011 Philip R. Yannella

Blackwell Publishing was acquired by John Wiley & Sons in February 2007. Blackwell's publishing program has been merged with Wiley's global Scientific, Technical, and Medical business to form Wiley-Blackwell.

Registered Office

John Wiley & Sons Ltd, The Atrium, Southern Gate, Chichester, West Sussex, PO19 8SQ, United Kingdom

Editorial Offices

350 Main Street, Malden, MA 02148-5020, USA

9600 Garsington Road, Oxford, OX4 2DQ, UK

The Atrium, Southern Gate, Chichester, West Sussex, PO19 8SQ, UK

For details of our global editorial offices, for customer services, and for information about how to apply for permission to reuse the copyright material in this book please see our website at www.wiley.com/wiley-blackwell.

The right of Philip R. Yannella to be identified as the author of this work has been asserted in accordance with the UK Copyright, Designs and Patents Act 1988.

Wiley also publishes its books in a variety of electronic formats. Some content that appears in print may not be available in electronic books.

Designations used by companies to distinguish their products are often claimed as trademarks. All brand names and product names used in this book are trade names, service marks, trademarks or registered trademarks of their respective owners. The publisher is not associated with any product or vendor mentioned in this book. This publication is designed to provide accurate and authoritative information in regard to the subject matter covered. It is sold on the understanding that the publisher is not engaged in rendering professional services. If professional advice or other expert assistance is required, the services of a competent professional should be sought.

Library of Congress Cataloging-in-Publication Data

Yannella, Philip.
    American literature in context after 1929 / Philip R. Yannella.
        p. cm. – (Literature in context)
    Continues the author's: American literature in context from 1865 to 1929.
    Includes bibliographical references and index.
    ISBN 978-1-4051-8599-8 (hardcover : alk. paper) – ISBN 978-1-4051-8600-1 (pbk. : alk. paper) 1. American literature–20th century–History and criticism. 2. National characteristics, American, in literature. 3. Literature and history–United States–History–20th century. I. Yannella, Philip. American literature in context from 1865 to 1929.
II. Title.
    PS221.Y36 2011
    810.9′358730904–dc22

2010009965

A catalogue record for this book is available from the British Library.

Set in 11/14pt Minion by Toppan Best-set Premedia Limited
Printed and bound in Malaysia by Vivar Printing Sdn Bhd

1 2011

For

Sook Kyung Kim

Contents

Timeline of Texts and Historical Events

Texts	Historical Events
1929. William Faulkner, *The Sound and the Fury* **1930.** Michael Gold, *Jews Without Money* Langston Hughes, *Not Without Laughter* Twelve Southerners, *I'll Take My Stand* John Dos Passos, *The 42nd Parallel* William Faulkner, *As I Lay Dying* **1931.** William Faulkner, *Sanctuary* **1932.** James T. Farrell, *The Young Lonigan* John Dos Passos, *1919* William Faulkner, *Light in August* **1933.** E. E. Cummings, *Eimi* Zora Neale Hurston, "The Gilded Six Bits"	**1929.** Stock market crash in October, triggering the Great Depression. **1932.** "Hunger March" at Ford Motor Works in Dearborn, Michigan. March on Washington, DC of World War I veterans seeking immediate pensions for their service. **1933.** 25% of Americans are unemployed (unemployment will continue to be consistently high until 1941).

Texts	Historical Events
	Franklin Delano Roosevelt becomes President and New Deal legislation begins to be passed (he will be re-elected in 1936, 1940, and 1944). 21st Amendment repeals 18th Amendment and Prohibition ends (though some states continue forms of prohibition under state laws).
1934. James T. Farrell, *The Young Manhood of Studs Lonigan* Langston Hughes, *The Ways of White Folks*	**1934.** Writer Upton Sinclair nearly wins the governorship of California as the candidate of the political movement "End Poverty in California." First American Writers' Congress held.
1935. *Proletarian Literature in the United States. An Anthology* Clifford Odets, *Waiting for Lefty* James T. Farrell, *Judgment Day* **1935–45.** Meridel Le Sueur, parts of *The Girl* (1978) appear in magazines from 1935 to 1945.	
1936. Carlos Bulosan, "Be American" John Dos Passos, *The Big Money* William Faulkner, *Absalom, Absalom!* Carl Sandburg, *The People, Yes* **1937.** Zora Neale Hurston, *Their Eyes Were Watching God* Younghill Kang, *East Goes West: The Making of an Oriental Yankee*	**1936.** The Communist Party of the USA (CPUSA) publishes *What Is Communism?* by its presidential candidate, Earl Browder, which lays out Communist positions on the issues of the day for the American electorate. **1936–37.** Congress of Industrial Organizations has significant successes at unionizing important parts of the American labor force.

Texts	Historical Events
1938. William Faulkner, "Barn Burning"	
1939. Pietro DiDonato, *Christ in Concrete*	
John Steinbeck, *The Grapes of Wrath*	
1940. Richard Wright, *Uncle Tom's Children*	
Richard Wright, *Native Son*	
William Faulkner, *The Hamlet*	
Budd Schulberg, *What Makes Sammy Run?*	
1941. Carlos Bulosan, "Homecoming"	
1942. William Faulkner, *Go Down, Moses*	
1943. Ayn Rand, *The Fountainhead*	**1943.** Repeal of Chinese Exclusion Act.
Jerre Mangione, *Mount Allegro*	
Eudora Welty, *The Wide Net*	
Wallace Stegner, *The Big Rock Candy Mountain*	
Eudora Welty, *Wide Net and Other Stories*	
1944. Richard Wright, "I Tried to be a Communist"	
1945. Tennessee Williams, *The Glass Menagerie*	**1945.** World War II in Europe ends.
	US atomic bombs the Japanese cities of Hiroshima and Nagasaki in August, leading to the end of the war in the Pacific.
	Press reports indicate that about 6 million Jews died during what will later be called the Holocaust.

Texts	Historical Events
	Nuremburg Trials of German war criminals and Tokyo trials of Japanese war criminals begin
	Press reports of widespread juvenile delinquency (such reports will continue in the ensuing years and decades).
1946. John Hersey, *Hiroshima* George Orwell, "Politics and the English Language" Ann Petry, *The Street*	**1946.** George Kennan writes blueprint for theory of "Containment" (of the Soviet Union).
	British Prime Minister Winston Churchill delivers his speech describing the "iron curtain" that has been erected by the Soviet Union across central and eastern Europe.
	1947. US House of Representatives Committee on Un-American Activities (HUAC) holds hearings on Communist influence in the motion picture industry; 10 screenwriters and directors receive Contempt of Congress citations, serve jail terms, and are later blacklisted from the industry.
	US produces about half of the world's manufactured goods.
	Construction begins on the first Levittown, in a Long Island suburb of New York City.

Texts	Historical Events
1948. Albert Deutsch, *The Shame of the States* Norman Mailer, *The Naked and the Dead* Ralph Ellison, "Harlem is Nowhere" (not published until 1964)	**1948.** Former State Department official Alger Hiss is accused of spying for the Soviet Union (later, he is convicted of perjury and goes to prison). International Congress on Mental Health convenes in London, at which the US Surgeon General reports that one-seventeenth of the US population is "psychotic" and that 10% of Americans will spend some portion of their lives in mental institutions.
1949. Richard Crossman (ed.) *The God That Failed* Langston Hughes and Arna Bontemps, *The Poetry of the Negro* Arthur Miller, *Death of a Salesman* Phyllis McGinley, "Suburbia, Of Thee I Sing" **1951.** J.D. Salinger, *The Catcher in the Rye* Rachel Carson, *The Sea Around Us* **1952.** Ralph Ellison, *Invisible Man*	**1949.** Soviet Union tests its first atomic bomb. China becomes a Communist state. HUAC begins publication of massively distributed propaganda pamphlets, *100 Things You Should Know About Communism.* Department of Justice begins prosecution of Communist Party leaders under the Alien Registration Act of 1940 (Smith Act). The film *Red Menace* is released, one of the earliest of a great number of anti-Communist films made in the ensuing years. **1950.** South Korea is invaded by Communist North Korea. Julius and Ethel Rosenberg and associates are indicted for spying for the Soviet Union.

Texts	Historical Events
1951. J.D. Salinger, *The Catcher in the Rye* Rachel Carson, *The Sea Around Us* **1952.** Ralph Ellison, *Invisible Man* **1953.** David Potter, *People of Plenty*	Republican Senator Joseph McCarthy makes a speech in which he says he has a list of 205 State Department employees who are Communists. Internal Security Act bars aliens who had been Communists in their home countries from entering US. **1953.** Senator Joseph McCarthy becomes Chairman of the Senate Committee on Government Operations and its Subcommittee on Investigations. McCarthy Committee launches probes of Communist influence on a number of government agencies, such as the United States Information Service (USIS) and the Voice of America, and on the Signal Corp of the US Army. Langston Hughes is subpoenaed by McCarthy to testify on the placement of 16 of his books in USIS libraries. 35% of the American workforce is unionized, an all-time high.
1954. Eudora Welty, "Place in Fiction"	**1954.** The US Supreme Court declares in *Brown v. Board of Education* that the doctrine of "separate but equal" is unconstitutional and that integration of schools should be accomplished "with all deliberate speed."

Texts	Historical Events
1955. Vladimir Nabokov, *Lolita* Flannery O'Connor, *A Good Man is Hard to Find* Sloan Wilson, *The Man in the Gray Flannel Suit* Rachel Carson, *The Edge of the Sea* **1956.** Gwendolyn Brooks, *Bronzeville Boys and Girls* Allen Ginsberg, *Howl and Other Poems* William H. Whyte, *The Organization Man* **1957.** William Faulkner, *The Town* James Baldwin, "Sonny's Blues" Norman Mailer, "The White Negro" Jack Kerouac, *On the Road* Bernard Malamud, *The Assistant* John Keats, *The Crack in the Picture Window* Loren Eiseley, *The Immense Journey* William Mann Dobriner, *The Suburban Community* **1958.** Howard Fast, *The Naked God: The Writer and the Communist Party* Tennessee Williams, *Suddenly Last Summer*	The Rosenbergs are executed (their associates serve prison terms). US Senate censures Senator McCarthy for bringing the Senate into "dishonor and disrepute." US Senate Subcommittee to Investigate Juvenile Delinquency begins hearings. **1956.** Soviet Premier Nikita Khrushchev gives speech in which he says his predecessor, Josef Stalin, committed a vast number of criminal acts, including the ordering of "mass repression" of Soviet citizens.

Texts	Historical Events
1959. John Cheever, "The Housebreaker of Shady Hill" William Faulkner, *The Mansion* Michael Harrington, "Our Fifty Million Poor" **1960.** Bernard Malamud, *The Magic Barrel* Paul Goodman, *Growing Up Absurd* Bennett Berger, *Working-Class Suburb* John Updike, *Rabbit Run* Philip Roth, *Goodbye, Columbus and Five Short Stories*	**1959.** Vice President Richard M. Nixon and Premier Nikita Khrushchev debate the merits of the capitalist and Communist systems at a trade show in Moscow.
1961. Lewis Mumford, *The City in History* Richard Yates, *Revolutionary Road* **1962.** Ken Kesey, *One Flew Over the Cuckoo's Nest* Betty Friedan, *The Feminine Mystique* Edward Albee, *Who's Afraid of Virginia Woolf* Rachel Carson, *Silent Spring* Michael Harrington, *The Other America* Herbert Gans, *The Urban Villagers*	**1961.** Freedom Rides in southern states led by Student Non-Violent Coordinating Committee (SNCC). **1962.** Students for a Democratic Society (SDS) founded.
1963. Flannery O'Connor, "The Regional Writer" Gwendolyn Brooks, *Selected Poems* Sylvia Plath, *The Bell Jar* James Baldwin, *The Fire Next Time*	**1963**. President John F. Kennedy assassinated.

Texts	Historical Events
1964. Hubert Selby, Jr., *Last Exit to Brooklyn* Amiri Baraka, *Dutchman* Dan Greenburg, *How To Be A Jewish Mother: A Very Lovely Training Manual*	**1964.** Free Speech Movement at the University of California at Berkeley. Students do community organizing and voter registration during "Mississippi Summer." Civil Rights Act of 1964 passed by Congress and signed by President. **1965.** Malcolm X assassinated. Voting Rights Act of 1965 passed by Congress and signed by President. President Johnson announces his administration will wage an "unconditional war on poverty." Hart–Celler Act regarding immigration abolishes national quotas.
1966. Truman Capote, *In Cold Blood* SNCC, "The Basis of Black Power" **1967.** Jerry Farber, "The Student as Nigger" Warren Hinckle, "A Social History of the Hippies" Herbert Gans, *The Levittowners* Norman Mailer, *Why Are We in Vietnam?* Robert Bly and David Ray (ed.), *A Poetry Reading Against the Vietnam War* **1968.** Eldridge Cleaver, *Soul on Ice*	**1965–67.** Riots and other civil disturbances in black areas of many cities. **1968.** Martin Luther King, Jr., assassinated. Robert Kennedy assassinated.

Texts	Historical Events
Norman Mailer, *The Armies of the Night*	Strike at San Francisco State University.
Naomi Jaffe and Bernadine Dohrn, "The Look is You: A Strategy for Radical Women"	National Advisory Commission on Civil Disorders explains recent city riots as mainly the
Tom Wolfe, *The Electric Kool-Aid Acid Test*	consequence of white racism, police brutality, the lack of
The Last *Whole Earth Catalog*	employment opportunities for
1969. Philip Roth, *Portnoy's Complaint*	blacks, and the deteriorated condition of many black
1970. H. Rapp Brown, *Die, Nigger, Die*	neighborhoods.
Robin Morgan, "Goodbye to All That"	
Robert Bly, "The Teeth Mother Naked at Last"	
James Dickey, *Deliverance*	
1971. Ann Petry, "The Witness"	**1971.** A study done at Cornell
Charles Bukowski, *Post Office*	University reports that the US
1973. Toni Morrison, *Sula*	has dropped 6.3 million tons of
1976. Norman Maclean, *A River Runs Through It*	aerial munitions on Laos, Cambodia, and Vietnam (during
1977. Michael Herr, *Dispatches*	WW II, the US dropped 2 million tons in all its operations).
1978. Andrew Macdonald, *The Turner Diaries*	**1978.** Partial core meltdown of nuclear reactor at Three Mile
1982. William Least Heat-Moon, *Blue Highways*	Island in Pennsylvania.
1985. Gretel Ehrlich, "The Solace of Open Spaces"	
1988. Bharati Mukherjee, *The Middleman and Other Stories*	
1996. Gish Jen, *Mona in the Promised Land*	

Texts	Historical Events
1997. Philip Roth, *American Pastoral* **1998.** Philip Roth, *I Married a Communist* Barry Lopez, *About This Life*	
	2000. Census indicates that as a result of the immigration reforms begun in the 1960s, about 10% of the American population is foreign-born.
2004. Philip Roth, *The Plot Against America* **2006**. Richard Ford, *The Lay of the Land* **2007**. Ha Jin, *A Free Life* Junot Diaz, *The Brief Wondrous Life of Oscar Wao* **2009**. Ha Jin, *A Good Fall*	**2009.** Pew Research Center estimates that about 11 million illegal immigrants live in the US (out of a population of 300 million).

Introduction

American Literature in Context after 1929 is intended to provide readers with basic knowledge about key, ongoing American social issues so that they can better understand literary texts. As in my *American Literature in Context from 1865 to 1929*, each chapter describes an issue and then discusses how it was engaged by representative writers. I do not attempt to provide an historian's hindsight perspective that utilizes a full array of evidence; rather, I present the issues as they might have been understood by writers at the times they were writing. The ongoing issues include the following: (1) how individuals are valued, how ordinary people fare in American society, and what opportunities exist for them; (2) the nature and role of the state and how it responds to real and perceived threats; (3) how the young respond to the world they will inherit; (4) how people are connected to one another and to the places in which they live; and (5) how newcomers fare in the US. Each of the five is absolutely fundamental. Each could generate encyclopedias of information, discussion, and debate – and has done so.

My account of the issues and their involvement in representative literary works is broad and brief. The first chapter is about the political and literary ferment of the Great Depression and World War II years, ending in a brief listing of the horrendous numbers of World War II deaths. It focuses on social change issues and the interest of many writers in so-called "ordinary people" or "everyday folk" as primary subjects. The second chapter is about anti-Communism, the overarching movement that determined many features of post-World War II American foreign and domestic policy and that also had a profound influence on American writing and on literary culture. Following a brief description of the postwar American economic boom, the third chapter describes widespread concern about the well-being of the nation's young people and the "discovery" that millions of Americans suffered from mental illness. Juvenile misbehavior and mental illness was explored – and sometimes celebrated – in major literary works. The chapter ends with some comments on 1960s youth radicalism and literature about the Vietnam War. The fourth chapter focuses on broad discussions of the values associated with city life, suburban life, rural life, the built environment, and the natural environment; issues regarding allegedly meaningless work as opposed to worthwhile work are discussed in this chapter because of the close association of place with work. The final chapter is a discussion of some examples of mid-century ethnic writing, an account of the 1965 legislative reopening of the country to large-scale immigration, and a discussion of some very recent writing by "new" immigrants.

In *American Literature in Context from 1865 to 1929*, I assumed that most of my readers had little knowledge of basic historical events and trends. Here, I assumed that readers have at least a working knowledge of the causes and consequences of World War II, the civil rights movement, the youth rebellions of the 1960s, and the causes and consequences of the Vietnam War. If some readers did not have that prior knowledge, I reasoned, they could easily get it through website articles and other commonly available resources.

The most intense period of social engagement by American writers began shortly after the stock market crash of 1929 and continued into the World War II years. After 1945, writers showed far less interest in wealth and poverty, power and powerlessness, the situations of ordinary workers, and so forth. One cause for this lessening of interest was the disaffection of many writers from politics because of the failures of Communism, the chief sponsor of engaged literature for more than two decades. A second cause was the developing sense in American literary culture that, as the English writer George Orwell put it in his widely read 1946 essay "Politics and the English Language," politics was "a mass of lies, evasions, folly, hatred, and schizophrenia" and that political engagement killed real art. But "politics" and "political" are elastic terms, as indicated by the wide acceptance of the idea that "the personal is political." As I hope to show, American writing after World War II was still deeply engaged, and not just at the personal level.

1

The Depression and the Early 1940s

The Context

From the Civil War through the 1920s, there was a great deal of poverty in the United States. Decades of protest, political agitation, and unionization efforts were not successful in altering basic economic conditions and the near-revolutionary agitation of the years between 1916 and 1919 ended in total loss for reformers, unionists, socialists, and other dissidents. The prosperity of the 1920s helped some people in some regions and economic sectors of the country. But all ships were not raised on the tide of prosperity; some economic sectors, including the large agricultural sector, continued to suffer.

The long-term problems of farmers were exacerbated during the 1930s by severe drops in the price of farm products and drops in consumer demand. Farming became an even more tenuous occupation than it had been, farm profits thinner, farm families less stable. Parts of the country were also struck by a multiyear drought. The hardest hit was the so-called Dust Bowl, a large area that included western Kansas, the southern edge of Nebraska, southeastern Colorado, the northwestern corner of Oklahoma, northwestern Texas, and the northeastern edge of New Mexico. Wind storms across the Dust Bowl carried away topsoil made vulnerable to erosion by poor farming practices, crops failed year after year, great numbers of farms went into foreclosure, and local economies were devastated.

Popular representations of 1930s farmland conditions sometimes make it seem that all except very wealthy farmers failed and left the land. In actuality, according to the occupational summaries of the 1930 and 1940 Censuses, the numbers of farmers and tenant farmers grew during the decade, from 5.0 million in 1930 to 5.1 million in 1940. The number of farm laborers, people who worked for wages on farms, however, declined from 4.4 to 3.0 million.

Of the 1930 American workforce of 49 million people, 21 percent worked in farming and 29 percent worked in one of the manufacturing/mechanical industries. As used by the Census, manufacturing/mechanical was a catch-all category. The majority in it were skilled craft workers, apprentices, engineers, builders, contractors, manufacturers, foremen, managers, and the like. Some 6.5 million people in the category – about 13 percent of the total workforce – were unskilled factory "operatives" and laborers; about half of those 6.5 million worked in the steel, auto, cotton, and clothing industries or as miners. Along with farm laborers, those unskilled operatives and laborers – together, these groups comprised one-fifth of the workforce – became the focus of government attention, renewed unionization drives, and later visual and written representations of the Great Depression.

Official government figures put unemployment at 25 percent in 1933, 21.7 percent in 1934, 20.1 percent in 1935, 16.9 percent in 1936, 14.3 percent in 1937, 19.0 percent in 1938, and 10 percent in 1941. The miseries triggered by unemployment – homelessness, hunger, broken families, forced migrations, and psychological traumas – were far worse and of far longer duration than the country experienced in any prior depression.

The Hoover Administration, which assumed office in early 1928, took the position that the Depression triggered by the stock market crash of October 1929 would end as soon as the "business cycle" went through a period of "self-correction." In the mounting strikes and protests of 1930 and 1931, the Administration did little to discourage businesspeople and their allies from responding with the same repressive measures that had been used for decades. In 1932, its responses to two large protests came to symbolize its attitudes. The first protest was the "Hunger March" at the Ford Motor Works in Dearborn, Michigan, protesting the layoffs of some 60,000 workers. That protest ended with police and Ford guards using tear gas and then shooting into crowds, killing four and wounding several dozen. The second protest was a march on Washington, DC, by World War I veterans demanding that the pensions they had been promised for their service be paid not in 1945, as scheduled, but immediately. Around 20,000 veterans and family members encamped in the city and, after several weeks, were finally evicted by the US Army, which used tanks, infantry formations, and tear gas to do the job.

Throughout the 1920s, American unions had great difficulties negotiating contracts and organizing new workers. After the stock market crash of 1929, those difficulties continued. During the Hoover years, there were renewed efforts to bring about unionization and equally forceful efforts by businesspeople to resist unionization which, from their perspectives, represented a fundamental challenge to private property rights and social order.

Franklin Delano Roosevelt took office in 1933 with altogether different beliefs than President Hoover about how to end the Depression. Roosevelt and the new Democratic-controlled Congress believed that the Federal government needed to take an active, aggressive role and intercede in the market-driven economy, including the labor market; that it needed to take a major role in planning for economic development; and that it needed to serve as an employer of last resort, putting people to work on publicly funded projects. In Roosevelt's first term, Congress passed major pieces of legislation – a "New Deal" for Americans – that put those beliefs into action. The government entered the marketplace as regulator and arbitrator through the Federal Emergency Relief Administration, the Agricultural Adjustment Administration, and the National Recovery Administration. It took its first steps toward endorsing the orderly development of labor unions in Section 7a of the National Recovery Act, which gave workers in some industries the right to organize unions while prohibiting coercion by employers. It took on a central planning role through the Tennessee Valley Authority, a government-owned corporation that was responsible for the redevelopment of the Tennessee Valley watershed that spanned seven southern states. It became the employer of last resort through the Civilian Conservation Corp and the Civil Works Administration. In 1935, Congress passed the Social Security Act, and the Works Project Administration (WPA), another government public works program that in later years employed numbers of artists and writers, was established. Also passed in 1935, the Wagner Act mandated that workers be free to select their own union; legalized striking, picketing, and boycotting; prohibited employer practices like black-listing; established the National Labor Relations Board (NLRB) to oversee the election of a union as an exclusive bargaining agent; and mandated that managements bargain in good faith with NLRB-certified unions. The Wagner Act put the Federal government squarely on the side of labor unions. New Deal legislation continued to be passed during Roosevelt's second term. In 1938, the Fair Standards Labor Act was passed. That legislation prohibited child labor, established a minimum wage, and established a 40-hour standard work week.

The cascade of early New Deal reforms did not immediately end the Depression. Continuing widespread misery was summarized in 1936 by President Roosevelt in the "Inaugural Address" that began his second term, when he spoke of the millions of people living "under conditions labeled indecent by a so-called polite society half a century ago," the millions "denied education, recreation, and the opportunity to better their lot and the lot of their children," and concluded that he saw "one-third of a nation ill-housed, ill-clad, ill-nourished."

The Wagner Act led to major drives by the new Committee for Industrial Organization (CIO) to unionize unskilled workers and others in the mass production industries. In late 1936 and early 1937, the CIO chose as its main target the largest American corporation, the auto manufacturer General Motors, reasoning that if it could unionize GM, other corporations would see that resistance was futile and would negotiate contracts. "Sitdown" strikes were used against GM. These involved workers taking control of the factories in which they worked by sitting down on the factory floor close to the machinery and refusing to leave until a contract was negotiated. The tactic was dramatic and new (though it had actually been used earlier in other strikes). Because the machinery could be damaged, the strikers were not exposed to attacks by company police, local police, and state militias.

GM's flagship production center in Flint, Michigan, was the central site for the sitdown strikers. Helped by the labor-friendly Roosevelt Administration and by the recently elected labor-friendly Governor of Michigan, Frank Murphy, the union won the Flint strike when GM agreed to recognize it and to negotiate a contract that would cover all auto workers at its plants. GM's capitulation demonstrated that the CIO had power and important allies. Most important, it led to successful union drives in other mass production industries and to a belief within the union movement that destiny was on its side and that more than one hundred years of resistance by American corporations to negotiating contracts with their workforces had come to an end.

The Hoover Administration had a "hands-off" approach to ending the Depression, while the Roosevelt Administration hoped to end it through basic reforms and employment programs. A number of other political parties and reform movements, both radical and conservative, were established or came into new prominence during the Great Depression. Most had little impact. A group called End Poverty in California, founded by the writer Upton Sinclair, came closest to actually gaining power when Sinclair won the Democratic primary for Governor in 1934 and seemed headed for victory until the leaders of the California Republican and Democratic Parties joined together to engineer his narrow defeat in what was called at the time "the campaign of the century." The group that had by far the deepest and most lasting impact was the Communist Party of the United States of America (CPUSA). Formed in 1919, the CPUSA had been small and largely ineffectual during the 1920s. But almost immediately after the stock market crash, because of its leadership in some strikes and protests, it began to make gains. By the time Roosevelt took office in 1933, it had a considerable presence in New York City and a few other places.

The CPUSA's impact was not to be measured in terms of how it did in elections, for it never attracted more than a microscopic number of voters. Rather, its impact was felt in other ways. First, of course, the CPUSA was the cause of anti-Communism, a transcending political and social movement, far more important than the CPUSA itself, which over its long history from the 1930s into the 1980s fundamentally shaped American domestic politics and foreign policy. Second, but most important for this and the next chapter, in its Great Depression heyday the CPUSA attracted a significant number of writers to its cause and thereby had a major impact on American literature. That impact included the production by writers of CPUSA literary works. It also led to the later targeting of writers as subversives by anti-Communists and was a cause of the depoliticization of American literature after 1950.

More so than other political parties, the CPUSA sometimes dramatically changed its positions. During the 1930s, the party's most notable shifts involved such questions as whether or not to cooperate with liberals and others, whether to damn or to enthusiastically support the New Deal, and whether significant change was destined to occur through revolution or through evolution. A person could be attracted to the Party in, say, 1930 by its positions on certain issues and discover a few years later that those positions were now deemed, in the party's standard language, "incorrect" and had been superseded by "correct" ones. Many such changes were mandated by the Communist International in the Soviet Union, a fact which, its opponents said, showed that American Communists were puppets who danced at the will of their Soviet puppeteers. The claim that Communists were puppets or agents of the Soviets, and that the Soviets were conspiring to subvert and destroy the US, would later develop into the foremost principle of anti-Communism.

Given its shifting stances, what did the CPUSA believe? In 1936, near the apex of its popularity, the party published a book titled *What Is Communism?*, written by Earl Browder. Browder held the top position of Secretary of the Party and was its presidential candidate; the book, an extended campaign guide and manifesto, stressed the following positions:

- The Soviet Union was the beacon of hope for humankind. In the less than 20 years after the Bolshevik Revolution, it had made astounding progress: "The revolution transformed the degraded masses into the rulers of the country. It raised their standards of living and created a new and wonderful life. In the Soviet Union a new kind of human being was being created, and there they are actually realizing the dream of all the best minds of history – socialism. ... The victory of socialism in the Soviet Union is the fruit of the genius of Stalin, who led the Communist Party and all Soviet toilers to their great triumph."[1]
- The Party promised that it would support progressive unions, social movements, and legislation that would enable the masses to survive the crisis of the Depression. The Depression, however, was in actuality the beginning of the end of capitalism, not a short-term crisis.
- Declaring that the US had been founded through revolution, the Party claimed that the "Declaration of Independence was for that time what the Communist Manifesto is for ours."[2] It said, "We Communists claim the revolutionary traditions of Americanism. We are the only ones who consciously continue those traditions and apply them to the problems of today. *We are the Americans and Communism is the Americanism of the twentieth century*" (italics in original).[3] At many of its large meetings, the speakers' platform was decked with American flags and "Yankee Doodle" was played. Abraham Lincoln was often invoked as a great inspiration.
- It argued that black Americans were "doubly oppressed," by race as well as by social class. It promised that it would work hard and tirelessly for the economic, political, and social equality of black Americans. The treatment of minorities in the Soviet Union would be emulated, for "the Soviet Union today is composed of 100 different nations and national

[1] Earl Browder, *What Is Communism?* (Vanguard Press, New York, 1936), pp. 213–14.
[2] *What Is Communism?* p. 16.
[3] p. 19

minorities. They live in harmony, and mutually aid each other's development."[4]

- It argued that "The fascist drive toward a second world war is gaining momentum"[5]: Italy had invaded Ethiopia, the Japanese imperialists had seized Manchuria and North China, and Japan and Germany would soon attack the Soviet Union. It promised that it would press the American government to counter the fascist threat, to end its policy of isolating the country from the rest of the world. It said it would petition Congress and the President "for the embargo of trade and loans against Italy and all other fascist aggressors,"[6] that it would organize mass meetings to protest fascist aggression, and that it would organize workers to take mass action against the aggressors.

- The US would become an altogether different country once Communism had triumphed. The government of "Soviet America," under the full control of the people, would immediately "take over and operate the banks, railroads, water and air transport, mines and all major trustified industries [i.e., monopolies]" as well as large-scale agriculture. Minor industries would be reorganized as "functions of local government or as cooperatives, or, in some instances, as auxiliaries of minor industries." Small farmers would be organized into cooperatives. All able-bodied people would be required to work for "socially determined" wages. As a result of productivity increases, the standard of living would be raised. People would live in decent housing and eat good food and be "liberated from regimented mental slavery to Hollywood, Hearst & Co."[7] Moreover, there would be a "full unfolding of the marvelous potentialities of the human spirit, the development of human genius and individuality raised to the nth power because it is no longer the power of a few individuals but of the masses of free men and women."[8]

[4] p. 188.
[5] p. 170.
[6] p. 179.
[7] pp. 228–30.
[8] p. 231.

There were other issues discussed in *What Is Communism?*, but the ones outlined above were those which apparently captured people's imaginations. Among all the CPUSA positions, its stance on the black American cause proved especially attractive, resonating with black writers like Langston Hughes, Richard Wright, and Ralph Ellison. The CPUSA efforts to organize sharecropper unions in southern states, to promote interracial relationships and marriages among its members and sympathizers, and its "special" efforts in Harlem in New York City, the so-called "black capital" of the US, were followed attentively by those and other writers.

To be an actual member of the Party, as opposed to a sympathizer or occasional supporter, an individual needed to subscribe to its program, to work actively under the direction of the Party, and to pledge to follow the Party's decisions. According to *What Is Communism?*, there were 7,000 members in 1930, 9,000 in 1931, 14,000 in 1932, 18,000 in 1933, 26,000 in 1934, and 30,000 in 1935. In its May 30, 1938 cover story on Earl Browder, *Time* magazine reported that the CPUSA had 65,000 members, about 30,000 of whom were in New York City (the City had for decades been seen by many Americans as an alien place full of foreigners; its disproportionate number of CPUSA members made it seem even more alien).[9] Not only was Party membership small, but for many people, it was also very temporary. Years later, the writer Howard Fast reported in his memoir *Being Red* (1990) that William Z. Foster, Browder's predecessor and successor as General Secretary, told him that between 1920 and 1950 "more than 600,000 men and women had signed party cards and had become members of the party – most of them leaving after varying lengths of time."[10]

The CPUSA sometimes claimed that its real strength lay not just with its actual members, the people it sometimes called its "revolutionary vanguard," but with voters alienated from the Republican and Democratic parties. Presidential election results did not bear this

---

[9]   This article is available online at http://www.time.com/time/magazine/article/ 0,9171,759763,00.html

[10]   Howard Fast, *Being Red* (Houghton Mifflin, Boston, 1990), p. 354.

out. In 1932, its presidential candidate received about 103,000 votes, three-tenths of one percent of the total cast; in 1936, Browder received about 79,000 votes, two-tenths of one percent of the total; and in 1940, Browder received about 49,000, somewhat less than one-tenth of one percent of the total. Browder's name was left off some state ballots in 1940 because he was under Federal indictment for passport violations, but there was no indication during that election that he would have done any better had the indictment not existed.

Actual membership and election results aside, the CPUSA argued it had many sympathizers. In *What Is Communism?*, Browder wrote that "Membership in mass organizations of various kinds, not affiliated to the party but in general sympathy with its program on the main issues of the day, numbers about 600,000." On "special issues," he said, such as unemployment insurance and social security, five million members of various organizations were working with it. At the time, these claims were probably little more than political puffery. But in the fierce anti-Communism of later years, the claim of having so having many sympathizers and such a deep involvement with social security and unemployment insurance legislation helped to convince some that basic New Deal legislation was inspired by Communism and, also, that great numbers of Communist sympathizers existed within the Roosevelt Administration.

The Literature

In Communist theory, skillful writers could play important roles in winning over the hearts and minds of the masses to the revolutionary cause. Reports exposing the oppressions of capitalism, pamphlets, speeches, stories, poems, and plays would speak truth and inspire men and women to action. In flattering words attributed to Josef Stalin, leader of the Soviet Union from 1924 to 1953, the writer was "the engineer of the human soul." Literature had been regarded by earlier American writers such as Upton Sinclair and John Reed as a weapon of class warfare. Those earlier writers were acknowledged by the CPUSA: Reed was honored when writers' clubs that the party sponsored were named the John Reed Clubs. But Communist writers saw their work as more deeply committed and more central to the world revolution than any preceding work.

The first prominent showcase for Communist writing was *Proletarian Literature in the United States: An Anthology.*[11] In his "Critical Introduction" to the book, the leading Marxist intellectual Joseph Freeman remarked on the fact that in past years there had been "abstract debates" about whether "the revolutionary movement of the proletariat could inspire a genuine art" but he claimed that now there were no doubts, at least among the "most progressive minds" of the country. Freeman also remarked that at the first American Writers' Congress in 1934 – having a conference of writers was itself a new idea – writers had met and talked with each other about "specific craft problems, general literary questions, and means of safeguarding culture from the menace of fascism and war. A literary congress was possible in this country only when in the writer's mind the dichotomy between poetry and politics had vanished, and art and life were fused." He was as confident about this as he was confident about the "historic path" that the working class was now following into the "new world."

Most of the writers showcased in *Proletarian Literature in the United States* are no longer read by anyone other than specialists. Those still read include John Dos Passos, James T. Farrell, Kenneth Fearing, Mike Gold, Langston Hughes, Muriel Rukeyser, Richard Wright, Meridel Le Sueur, and Clifford Odets.

Much CPUSA writing tried to advance the revolution by teaching readers about the suffering of the people, first stating the cause of that suffering and then proclaiming an improved future. Poetry was ideally suited to this program, just as songs had been suited to the IWW program of earlier years, because a poem could rapidly simplify and summarize issues in memorable language. In slightly more than one hundred sharply detailed lines, for example, Tillie Olsen's

[11]   Granville Hicks, Joseph North, Michael Gold, Paul Peters, Isidor Schneider, Alan Calmer (eds), *Proletarian Literature in the United States: An Anthology* (International Publishers, New York, 1935).

"I Want You Women Up North to Know" described the painful lives of three exploited Latina women in San Antonio, Texas. In "Goodbye Christ," Langston Hughes, who became a master of this sort of direct but lyrical statement, asserted that Christ had been displaced by a "real guy" named "Marx Communist Lenin Peasant Stalin Worker ME," while in "Air Raid Over Harlem" he wrote a scenario for revolution in the black capital. Michael Gold's *Jews Without Money* (1930), a short autobiographical novel, worked through quick but evocative descriptions of characters and events.

Plays like Clifford Odets's short *Waiting for Lefty* (1935) were also good vehicles for Communist messages. Requiring no stage and no scenery, it was performed in many cities by amateur groups and before long was recognized as one of the great examples, perhaps the primary example, of the power of literature as a weapon. *Waiting for Lefty* taught audiences fundamental Communist beliefs about capitalism: that big business was totally focused on profit and was not "sentimental over human life," that it thought consumers were helpless sheep, that it manufactured poison gas for profit, that it liked its skilled workers to stay sober but wanted its "Pollacks and niggers" to drink because drinking "keeps them out of mischief," and that it tried to destroy unions and divide the working class. It incorporated standard Communist perceptions about corrupt, well-fed union leaders who held their membership back from radical action and "sleeping" workers who did not yet understand their actual class positions. Capturing the energy and spirit of mid-1930s unionization drives, the ultimate message of *Waiting for Lefty* was that sleeping workers could be awakened and then be rapidly radicalized to take collective action by striking for a "new world" and, if necessary, by dying for "what is right."

Communist literature often depicts people willing to die for the cause. That zeal is at the center of Richard Wright's "Bright and Morning Star," one of the five stories in *Uncle Tom's Children* (1940) and probably the Communist story that continues to be most read. The backdrop to the story was the CPUSA effort to organize black and white poor people in the rural South and the violent opposition of white communities. The heroine of the story, Aunt Sue, has raised two sons who became Communists and through them her old Christian vision of the world had been "ripped from her startled eyes" and replaced with a Communist vision, expressed in the language of Christianity, that was "great and strong enough to fling her into the light of another grace" and in which the "meager beginnings of the party had become another Resurrection." Among the Communists, differences of race had been pushed aside; as one of her sons says, "Ah cant see white n Ah cant see black ... Ah sees rich men n Ah sees po men." At the end of the story, Aunt Sue and one of her sons, Johnny-Boy, go to their deaths at the hands of the local sheriff but not before Aunt Sue, full of "pride and freedom," kills the Judas-like Booker who is about to inform the sheriff of the names of other Communists. The police, of course, are revealed to be ignorant and gratuitously inhumane.

Wright's other major achievement during his 1933–42 Communist phase was *Native Son* (1940), a novel that brilliantly depicts the horrifying ghetto conditions of black Chicago and their effects on the 19-year-old Bigger Thomas. Bigger commits two murders. The murder of Mary Dalton, a wealthy young white woman who is involved with a young Communist, is seemingly accidental but produces elation in Bigger; the murder of his girlfriend is premeditated. A fast-paced novel of crime and punishment, packed with extraordinary descriptive passages about the cruelties of racism, *Native Son* was a best seller. Some contemporary critics also claimed that it was the most important novel ever written by an American black writer. For non-Communist readers, it no doubt served to provide – especially those parts in which Bigger's lawyer Boris A. Max explains to Bigger what, from a Communist point of view, he actually did and why he did it – an instructional manual on how Communists thought about the world and a series of brilliant insights into the causes of black anger. For many Communist readers, of course, *Native Son* demonstrated the power of literature to represent and to inspire.

Literature which directly attacked Communist ideology, and literature which argued for conservative, individualistic, anarchistic, or libertarian positions, was also published in the 1930s and 1940s. The several southern writers and intellectuals who contributed to the

1930 collection of essays *I'll Take My Stand* argued for a rejection of "progressive" industrial culture and collectivism while maintaining that "the culture of the soil is the best and most sensitive of vocations, and ... it should have the economic preference and enlist the maximum number of workers." In the left-dominated literary culture of the 1930s, *I'll Take My Stand* was almost universally regarded as retrograde and racist. Similar treatment was given E. E. Cummings's *Eimi* (1933), a journal of the author's trip to Russia in which he recorded his astonishment at the repressive, totalitarian, inhumane "unworld" of the Soviet Communist "hell." Cummings's book was met mostly with silence. But the Modernist writer Ezra Pound thought it was a major literary work. Pound, who had lived in Italy for many years and supported the fascist side in World War II, made more than one hundred pro-fascist broadcasts on Italian radio during the war. Most of them were rants against Jews, Roosevelt, liberals, Communists, and others, but during his May 21, 1942 broadcast, he held *Eimi* out as the sort of book ignorant Americans should read instead of the usual "blah about democracy, freedom, baloney."[12] (After the war, the government arrested Pound for treason and brought him back to the US to stand trial. Pound was ultimately committed to a mental institution.)

Ayn Rand's *The Fountainhead* (1943) was the most widely read and influential literary work that argued for the individualistic as opposed to the "collectivist" (socialist and/or Communist) view of human destiny. Mostly popularized by word of mouth – mainstream literary culture dismissed it in the 1940s and continues to dismiss it – the book sold hundreds of thousands of copies and by the 1950s had become a central text of American conservative and libertarian political culture.

The Fountainhead contains a critique of collectivism, much of it accomplished through the characterization of Ellsworth M. Toohey, a sexless, Harvard-educated socialist who makes his living as a highly regarded art and architecture critic. Toohey speaks with authority

---

[12] Pound's radio speeches are collected in Leonard W. Doob (ed.), *"Ezra Pound Speaking": Radio Speeches of World War II* (Greenwood Press, Westport, CT, 1978).

about "strikes, and conditions in the slums, and the poor people in sweatshops" and he sounds very much like a CPUSA leader when he tells strikers that "History, my friends, does not ask questions or acquiescence. It is irrevocable." He aims through his work to kill individualism, to destroy individual expression and creativity by preaching other-directed altruism, and to exalt the masses. Rand's basic critique of collectivism is expressed near the end when her main character, Howard Roark, tells a jury that "The 'common good' of a collective – a race, a class, a state – was the claim and justification of every tyranny ever established over men. Every major horror of history was committed in the name of an altruistic motive." Roark was being tried for blowing up the low-income housing project he had designed because, in violation of his agreement, its design had been modified; the jury acquits him, which is to say that the jury understands the integrity of the true artist.

In *The Fountainhead*, all of the major and many of the minor characters are measured by the work they do. Toohey works at destroying the egos, the souls of other men. The newspaper publisher Gail Wynand works to prove that the masses of men and women are venal, dumb, and easily bought. The architects in the novel – it can be read as a novel partly about the profession of architecture – are judged by the buildings they produce. The men who teach at the college of architecture Roark attends and is expelled from just before graduation, are out-of-date and inept. The architect Guy Francon imitates traditional styles for his wealthy clients. The hopelessly uncreative architect Peter Keating fakes his work. Henry Cameron, a character based on the architect Louis Sullivan, is committed to his work, believing that "Architecture is not a business, but a crusade and a consecration to a joy that justifies the existence of the earth." The heroic Howard Roark, whose character is based on the architect Frank Lloyd Wright, is given many speeches by Rand in which he talks about his work. Among other things, he says that the meaning of life is to be found in work, that he became an architect because he loves the world but does not like the way things are shaped and wants to change them, and that his work is his joy. In one speech, he philosophizes on what buildings represent:

> Most people build as they live – as a matter of routine and sense-less accident. But a few understand that a building is a great symbol. We live in our minds, and existence is the attempt to bring that life into physical reality, to state it in gesture and form. For the man who understands this, a house he owns is a statement of his life.

To indicate the outcomes of this philosophy, Rand provides several descriptions of the magnificent Modernist buildings Roark produces. But he is not a precious aesthete. Throughout the novel, Rand reminds readers that Roark was born into the working class, that he is largely self-educated, and that he knows how to do hard physical labor. Roark's close friend Mike, a skilled construction worker, has attitudes similar to Roark's, suggesting that true working-class heroes think of work as the highest form of self-expression: "People meant very little to Mike, but their performance a great deal. He worshipped expertness of any kind. He loved his work passionately and had no tolerance for anything save for other single-track devotions. He was a master in his own field and he felt no sympathy except for mastery."

Many important political and cultural figures have testified to the influence of *The Fountainhead* on them. Most recently, Cal Ripkin, who holds the record for the number of baseball games played without missing one, remarked that he, too, had tried to get fulfillment through his work, that he had been drawn to Rand's books, and that he had thought a good deal about Howard Roark.[13]

The Fountainhead also has a literary cultural dimension that satirizes both avant-garde writing and Communist writing. Among his other positions, Toohey is the leader of a group of avant-garde writers that includes a woman, Lois Cook, who, sounding like Gertrude Stein, says things like "It is so commonplace ... to be understood by everybody" and about whom Rand is cruelly satirical in remarks like "For an author who did not sell, her name seemed

---

[13]   Ray Robinson, "The Iron Horse and Ripkin," *New York Times*, July 29, 2007, p. SP5.

strangely famous and honored. She was the vanguard of intellect and revolt." Cook is also chairperson of the Council of American Writers, which believed that "writers were servants of the proletariat," though on some occasions the members talked more about "the tyranny of reality and of the objective" than about the proletariat. The group includes:

> a woman who never used capitals in her books, and a man who never used commas; a youth who had written a thousand-page novel without a single letter o, and another who wrote poems that neither rhymed nor scanned; a man with a beard, who was sophisticated and proved it by using every unprintable four-letter word in every ten pages of his manuscript ...

Details like those seemed to be calculated to alienate literary people enthusiastic about "experimental" writing as well as enthusiasts about Communist writing.

Ayn Rand's work aside, much of the engaged literature produced in the 1930s and early 1940s focused on the lives of "ordinary" or "everyday" Americans. Some had a CPUSA perspective, some were liberal and "progressive," and nearly all shared the view that the country was unfair and that the "People" suffered. This was a renewal of the interest of earlier writers in those they called "ordinary" or "undistinguished," an interest which crested between 1900 and 1919 in investigations of worker experience by journalists and in the fiction and poetry of writers such as Upton Sinclair, Jack London, and Carl Sandburg. In the 1930s and in the World War II years, however, the concern with the situation of the "People" was not just literary and journalistic. A great number of popular movies, such as those of Frank Capra, were made that exalted common men and women. The Roosevelt administration through the WPA sent photographers, artists, and writers out to discover and to record the lives of the people and the cultures of local communities. Some of the most distinguished work was focused on the South. A panoramic view of rural poverty was presented in *Let Us Now Praise Famous Men* (1940), which featured meditative prose by James Agee and photographs by Walker Evans. In the early 1940s, the writer Sterling A. Brown, without government funding, began a project to investigate and report on black life in the southern countryside. Brown published a few pieces of his study, but recently, John Edgar Tidwell and Mark A. Sanders edited Brown's preserved manuscripts into *Sterling A. Brown's A Negro Looks at the South* (2007), a masterful descriptive analysis of rural black life.

There was a world of great books and stories full of textured, detailed, skilled representations of the lives lived by ordinary people. Meridel Le Sueur's short stories focused on women, many of them unemployed. Her short novel *The Girl* was one of the period's great representations of the lives of working-class women during the depths of the Depression; the book was not published until 1978 but parts appeared in magazines between 1935 and 1945. Sherwood Anderson's "Death in the Woods," a 1933 short story, narrated the life of a farm woman exploited and victimized by men and her end in a strange kind of beauty that haunts the narrator for decades. Carl Sandburg's long poem *The People, Yes* (1936) was a gifted and strange compendium of facts and fictions and folk wisdom. James T. Farrell's *Studs Lonigan* trilogy, made up of *Young Lonigan* (1932), *The Young Manhood of Studs Lonigan* (1934), and *Judgment Day* (1935), is a virtual documentary of Irish-American working-class life in Chicago. Pietro DiDonato's *Christ in Concrete* (1939) narrates the lives as exploited labor lived by New York Italian-American construction workers and their families. Budd Schulberg's *What Makes Sammy Run?* (1941) asks all the fundamental questions about the motivations of Sammy Glick to become rich, powerful, and famous no matter what he has to do and supplies some answers in the form of its brief but luminous account of his Lower East Side Jewish upbringing; the unionization efforts of Hollywood screenwriters serves as part of the backdrop for Glick's rise. Nonfiction accounts of immigrant life published during the period included Carlos Bulosan's 1936 "Be American" and 1941 "Homecoming," Younghill Kang's *East Goes West: The Making of an Oriental Yankee* (1937), and Jerre Mangione's *Mount Allegro* (1943). Bulosan was from the Philippines and Kang was from Korea. Mangione was born in the US to Sicilian parents.

John Steinbeck's panoramic *The Grapes of Wrath* (1939) had the deepest lasting impact on American cultural history. It provided some iconic moments – for example, the images of the hardscrabble lives of southwestern tenant farmers during the 1930s drought, the Joad family trip across the Southwest in search of work, Tom's speech as he leaves the family to take up a life of union organizing, Ma Joad's speech about the endurance of the people – that still move readers. But many other great panoramic fictions appeared in this period. Wallace Stegner's *The Big Rock Candy Mountain* (1943) begins in the 1890s and ends during the 1930s, capturing the life of Bo Mason as he and his family live through hard times and occasional good times in North Dakota, Saskatchewan, Canada, the upper edges of the Northwest, Salt Lake City, and Lake Tahoe, Nevada. Bo Mason's work life seeking the big break and the big money is laid out in extraordinary detail in the novel, as are the landscapes and local cultures. An even larger panoramic book written in the period was John Dos Passos's brilliant trilogy *USA*, comprising *The 42nd Parallel* (1930), *1919* (1932), and *The Big Money* (1936). Dos Passos follows a group of representative characters through the first three decades of the twentieth century, juxtaposing their stories against tangles of news headlines, brief but uncannily accurate biographies of major cultural figures, and subthemes having to do with labor– management relations. In *The Grapes of Wrath*, unionization is also a major element, while *The Big Rock Candy Mountain* has no such dimension (Bo and Elsa Mason have no political consciousness, never even voting in an election).

Some of the sharpest writing of the period was by southerners. Zora Neale Hurston's 1926 short story "Sweat" was an early example of what developed in her work as a very full representation of black life in central Florida. Her 1933 story "The Gilded Six Bits," her novel *Their Eyes Were Watching God* (1937), and a number of her folklore studies – Hurston was a trained anthropologist – presented readers with nuanced, textured depictions of town and domestic life in a part of the country that had always been remote, mysterious, and subject to ridicule. Eudora Welty's early stories, the first collections of which were published in 1941 and 1943, represented mostly white folk

going about their mundane daily business in the Mississippi countryside and small towns. As in much of Hurston – but not the
Hurston in stories like "Sweat" – excitement and stimulation came
to Welty's characters in very small doses. In stories like "The Wide
Net" and "A Worn Path," life unfolded in day-to-day routines and
rituals; as Welty represented them, to ordinary people the world was
a magic place full of hazards that could be overcome by perseverance
and luck. Rational thought, logical analysis, and the rules of cause
and effect rarely existed. There was virtually no influence of national
events – the economy had always been and continued to be depressed
– and there was certainly no discussion whatsoever about jobs and
joblessness, labor unions, New Deal legislation, the historic destinies
of the proletariat, the rise of fascism, and so forth.

William Faulkner's amazingly productive period from 1929 to the
early 1940s included several novels absorbed with the never-ending
effects of slavery and the Civil War, family and kinship, race and
social relationships. His major work of this period – *The Sound and
the Fury* (1929), *As I Lay Dying* (1930), *Sanctuary* (1931), *Light in
August* (1932), *Absalom, Absalom!* (1936), *The Hamlet* (1940), and
Go Down, Moses (1942) – represented the southern present as a
consequence of its past and its various historical themes as profoundly and complexly entangled. Inevitably, not so much because
it was Depression-era writing but because it was set in Mississippi,
the most impoverished of states for much of its history, it was also
absorbed with matters of poverty and wealth, the ways people coped
and sometimes achieved a measure of dignity and fulfillment, and
the social processes by which some powerful families declined and
others rose in the twentieth century.

As I Lay Dying was as ambitious an attempt to extensively represent the thought processes and preoccupations of poor country
people as any published in the era. *Light in August*, aside from its
brilliant renderings of human consciousness, contained convincing
representations of rural folk culture and, at the end, in the character
of Percy Grimm, something of the feel of early 1920s crazed patriot-
ism and racism. *The Hamlet*, a sometimes comic representation of
country folk, began Faulkner's extensive treatment of the rise of the

fiercely acquisitive Snopes family, which he later completed in
The Town (1957) and *The Mansion* (1959).

"Barn Burning" is an often reprinted 1938 short story featuring
Ab Snopes, one of the family's progenitors. Set in the mid-1890s, it
distills many of Faulkner's themes about the situations of Mississippi
poor white folk in the nineteenth century and beyond. The poverty
of the Ab Snopes family is clear. They are tenant farmers who move
frequently. The barefoot boys of the family are unschooled and work
endlessly at farm jobs; the young girls of the family are described as
emanating "an incorrigible idle inertia." Hunger is alluded to in the
first paragraph and later, domestic violence perpetrated or threatened by Ab occurs regularly, fear of Ab is constantly present among
family members. Clear, too, is Ab's understanding of his enslave-
ment: as he is going to talk to the man for whom he is to sharecrop,
he says, "I reckon I'll have a word with the man that aims to begin
to-morrow owning my body and soul for the next eight months."

As in much of the major writing of the 1930s, class antagonism
runs deeply through "Barn Burning." Ab is a fearsome presence in
the farming communities through which he passes because, burning
the barns of his antagonists, he destroys one of the fundamental
sources of their livelihoods and wealth. These economic attacks,
farmland analogues to the sabotage, strikes, and other job actions
expressing class antagonism in industrialized parts of the country in
the 1930s as at other times, is of course seen as despicable by those
who attend courtroom sessions and function as members of a chorus
voicing conventional community values. At the end of the story, Ab
is killed while trying to commit another attack. But the narrator
seems to exalt Ab's character, referring to his "wolflike independence
and even courage" at one point and at another referring to his understanding of fire "as the one weapon for the preservation of integrity."
Comments like that might cause some readers to think of Ab as a
sort of proletarian hero, to use the language of the CPUSA. Those
details, however, are balanced by others that make Ab seem mean-
minded, gratuitously destructive, and confused: his service in the
Civil War motivated by his interest in accumulating booty; his war
wound received when he was shot by one of his fellow Confederate

soldiers while stealing a horse; his naming of his youngest son for the Colonel under whom he served in the war, despite his hostility to authority and the upper class; his destruction of his "owner's" valuable rug by first stomping horse manure deep into its fibers and then cleaning it with corrosive lye; and his blunt racism (shared by others in the story).

The last two paragraphs show the young boy Colonel Sartoris Snopes leaving the family and beginning to remember his father as a brave hero in the ceremonial language of late nineteenth-century Civil War memorials. We, though, as readers, know a lot more than the boy about Ab's real character as a soldier and about what his impoverished life has caused him and his family to become.

A Note on World War II Deaths

There were an estimated 22 to 25 million military deaths world-wide in World War II. The death toll included 9 to 11 million Soviet soldiers, 5.5 million Germans, 3 to 4 million Chinese, and 2.1 million Japanese. Nearly 417,000 American soldiers died.

There were an estimated 34 to 47 million civilian deaths worldwide. That death toll included 12 to 14 million Soviet citizens, 7 to 16 million Chinese, 3 to 4 million Indonesians, 2.5 million Poles, and 1.0 to 2.8 million Germans. Some 1,700 US civilians died.

Between 5.1 and 6 million Jews died in the Holocaust. During their occupations of other Asian countries, it was estimated that the Japanese killed somewhere between 13 and 26 million civilians (those numbers include the Chinese and Indonesians civilian deaths listed above).

In the spring of 1945, the US began to firebomb Japanese cities, killing hundreds of thousands of civilians in the process. Firebombing involved the dropping from low altitudes of incendiary devices intended to create huge, all-consuming fires.

In early August 1945 the US dropped atomic bombs on the Japanese cities of Hiroshima and Nagasaki. It was estimated that the Hiroshima bomb immediately killed some 70,000 to 140,000 civilians, while the Nagasaki bomb immediately killed some 70,000. More deaths occurred later from serious injuries and radiation sickness.

In the immediate aftermath of the war, Americans saw photos and film footage of the liberated German concentration camps and equally appalling photos and film of some victims of the Japanese. There were also detailed reports of war atrocities during the 1945 and 1946 Nuremburg Trials of German war criminals and the Tokyo trials of Japanese war criminals. The Hiroshima and Nagasaki atomic bombings were the subjects of a great deal of newspaper and magazine discussion in the first two years after the war ended. Very early, there were American and worldwide discussions of whether the bombings were necessary and whether they violated conventions on the conduct of war.

John Hersey's *Hiroshima*, published as the entire August 31, 1946 issue of the *New Yorker* and shortly afterwards as a book, which narrated the experience of six individuals who lived through the bombing, was the most widely read and influential of all the early postwar accounts.

2
Anti-Communism

The Context

During its Great Depression heyday, the Communist Party of the USA (CPUSA) argued that capitalism was dying and that a new economic and social model for humankind existed in the Soviet Union. That country, founded after the Bolshevik Revolution of 1917, had rapidly modernized under its centralized economy, creating, it was claimed, stunning economic progress and equality for its citizens. The Soviet Union was, according to the CPUSA, the world's most important and fiercest antifascist state and was also a place where there was no discrimination against ethnic and racial minorities. Portraying itself as the American arm of the impending international revolution, the CPUSA aimed to create an antifascist, egalitarian "Soviet America."

As we have seen, helping black Americans to achieve full equality was a major part of the CPUSA agenda. In that regard, among other initiatives, it tried to organize sharecroppers' unions in southern states, it promoted interracial relationships and marriages among its members and sympathizers, and it organized educational and social programs in black neighborhoods in major cities. Harlem in New York City, the so-called "black capital" of the US, was the site of some of its strongest efforts. What is now sometimes called the "long civil rights movement," as opposed to the civil rights movement of the 1950s and 1960s, began with the CPUSA.

American anti-Communists of the 1930s had an entirely different understanding of the Soviet Union and Communism. To them, the Soviet Union was a repressive, murderous state that was intent on erasing individualism and freedom and American Communists were either well-meaning but naïve dupes or, more likely, haters of freedom. Anti-Communists claimed that labor unions and all New Deal reform efforts were inspired by Communism. They also claimed that Communism was an elitist, and largely Jewish, "un-American" anomaly. To make this case, they pointed to the fact that among CPUSA followers were a significant number of intellectuals, theatre and film people, visual artists, and writers, a disproportionate number of whom were Jews.

Anti-Communism abated somewhat in the early 1940s because the United States and the Soviet Union were allies in World War II. But after the war ended in August 1945, and in direct response to the postwar Soviet creation of satellite states in eastern and central Europe, anti-Communism flared and quickly became the major theme of American political discourse.

In February 1946, George Kennan, an American diplomat in the Soviet Union, responded to some State Department questions about the nature of the Soviet regime and its intentions by sending a 5,300-word telegram to Secretary of State James Byrnes. Kennan's telegram, later published in the July 1947 issue of *Foreign Affairs*, the major journal of the American foreign policy profession, became a blueprint for American policy toward the Soviet state for decades to come. It included basic statements about Soviet devotion to Marxism-Leninism. It included an analysis of how Soviet leaders had never completed the process of "political consolidation" and thus perpetually struggled "to secure and make absolute the power which they seized in November 1917." It included an assertion that under its current leader, Joseph Stalin, "all internal opposition forces … have consistently been portrayed as the agents of foreign forces antagonistic to Soviet power" and, as a result, were suppressed by the army and the secret police. It included a statement on the Soviet belief in Communist Party "infallibility," the theory that the Communist Party leadership was the "sole repository of truth." Regarding future US policy toward the totalitarian Soviet Union, Kennan proposed "long-term, patient but firm and vigilant containment of Russian expansive tendencies."

Other Western leaders also believed that the Soviet Union was a repressive and expansionist totalitarian state. On March 5, 1946, two weeks after Kennan sent his long telegram, British Prime Minister Winston Churchill, speaking at Westminster College in Fulton, Missouri, said that "A shadow has fallen upon the scenes so lately lighted by the Allied victory. Nobody knows what Soviet Russia and its Communist international organization intends to do in the immediate future, or what are the limits, if any, to their expansive and proselytizing tendencies." Using a descriptive phrase that would be used for more than four decades, Churchill said:

> an iron curtain has descended across the Continent. Behind that line lie all the capitals of the ancient states of Central and Eastern Europe. Warsaw, Berlin, Prague, Vienna, Budapest, Belgrade, Bucharest and Sofia, all these famous cities and the populations around them lie in what I must call the Soviet sphere, and all are subject in one form or another, not only to Soviet influence but to a very high and, in some cases, increasing measure of control from Moscow.

The belief that there were two worlds, one free and the other savagely imprisoned behind an iron curtain, was the premise of American foreign policy from the 1940s through the 1980s, that is, for the entire period of what came to be called the Cold War. Throughout this period containment was the most fundamental element of American policy toward the Soviet Union.

The threat of a Communist takeover of the world mounted in the first years after the war. The Soviet Union consolidated its power in its satellite states in the late 1940s. In August 1949, it tested its first atomic bomb, thus bringing to an end the American monopoly on nuclear weapons. A few weeks later, on October 1, after a long civil war in which the United States supported the losing side, China became a Communist state allied with the Soviet Union. A short time later, border clashes began between Communist North Korea, an ally of the Soviet Union and China, and South Korea, an American ally. In June 1950, North Korea conducted a full-scale invasion of the

South, which in turn led to the commitment of substantial numbers of American troops under United Nations auspices and then, after the Americans routed the North Korean army and entered the North, the commitment by China of several hundred thousand "volunteer" troops. This is a quick summary of a few major postwar events. It leaves out a great number of other events on other fronts in the late 1940s and early 1950s, virtually all of which fueled the belief that the US and its allies were locked in a dangerous and potentially apocalyptic battle with the Soviet Union and its allies.

American Communists were seen as the allies and agents of the Soviets. Very few American politicians – whether conservative, centrist, or liberal – ever expressed any sympathy for the First Amendment rights of members of the CPUSA to create its "Soviet America." Anti-Communism became an article of faith subscribed to by virtually all politicians.

Anti-Communism of the postwar era unfolded on three major fronts. First, there were hearings held by the US House of Representatives Committee on Un-American Activities (HUAC). Second, there were prosecutions of Communists under the Smith Act, passed by Congress in 1940. Third, beginning in 1952 and continuing into early 1954, and simultaneous with HUAC hearings and Smith Act prosecutions, there were the hearings conducted by the US Senate Committee on Government Operations and its Subcommittee on Investigations, under the chairmanship of Senator Joseph McCarthy, Republican of Wisconsin. In addition, Communists and their allies were also vigorously pursued by state and local politicians, boards of education, police departments, and private employers.

HUAC had been established in 1937 to investigate disloyalty and subversion. With subpoena power to compel people to testify, the ability to get Contempt of Congress citations that carried penalties of imprisonment and fines against those who refused to testify, a considerable staff, solid funding, and the help of the Federal Bureau of Investigation (FBI), HUAC focused on Communist influence on the life of the nation. Its most famous moment came in October 1947, when it held nine days of hearings on Communist influence in the Hollywood motion picture industry. Films, HUAC members reasoned, could be used by their makers to propagandize mass audiences into sympathy for the Soviet Union or into other subversive, "un-American" beliefs. That there was indeed Communist influence on the film industry was supported by the testimony of such important industry figures as the President of the Screen Actors' Guild, Ronald Reagan, who would become the US President in 1980; the actors George Murphy and Robert Montgomery; the director Elia Kazan; the studio heads Walt Disney, Jack L. Warner of Warner Brothers, and Louis B. Mayer of Metro-Goldwyn-Mayer; and the screenwriter and novelist Ayn Rand.

Ten screenwriters and directors, later known as the "Hollywood 10," were targeted in the 1947 hearings. Refusing to cooperate with the Committee, to talk about their political beliefs, or to name other people they knew to be Communists, each of the 10 received Contempt of Congress citations and served jail terms. During his testimony, Eric Johnson, the President of the industry-wide Motion Picture Association of America, had argued for self-regulation by the industry and complained about HUAC's excesses and the creation of irrational fear in the country. A month after the hearings ended, Johnson recognized the tidal strength of anti-Communism and announced that his organization would no longer allow Communists to be employed in the industry and would suspend or fire each of the Hollywood 10. "Blacklisting" had long been a device used by managers of factories and mines to rid their industries of union agitators and radicals. Blacklisting from the film industry was the first step in what would become widespread blacklisting of entertainers and writers said to be Communists or Communist sympathizers ("fellow travelers" or "pinkos" in the language of the day). In later years, because they refused to answer questions about their political beliefs – typically, uncooperative witnesses argued that, in fact, HUAC was itself un-American because it violated the political and intellectual freedom Americans were guaranteed by the Constitution and Bill of Rights – people like the folksinger Pete Seeger, the playwright Lillian Hellman, and the singer/actor Paul Robeson were also blacklisted. Robeson's passport was taken away by the Committee, as was the passport of playwright Arthur Miller, though both later had their passports returned to them through a US Supreme Court decision.

Through much of the later 1940s and 1950s, important magazines and newspapers followed the HUAC pathway to proclaim this or that famous person a Communist or Communist sympathizer. A good example of this can be seen in an article in *Life* magazine in April, 1949 in which, reporting on a Cultural and Scientific Conference for World Peace held in Manhattan, the magazine published pictures of American "Dupes and Fellow Travelers" who attended. Among them were writers Dorothy Parker, Langston Hughes, Clifford Odets, Norman Mailer, Thomas Mann, William Rose Benet, Louis Untermeyer, George Seldes, and Lillian Hellman, composers Aaron Copeland and Leonard Bernstein, actor Charlie Chaplin, and scientist Albert Einstein. The magazine *did* say that "Some of those pictured here publicly and sincerely repudiate Communism," though it added that "this does not alter the fact that they are of great use to the Communist cause."[1]

HUAC usually targeted famously influential people who had been members or sympathizers of the CPUSA, thus assuring public interest and, as a by-product, free political advertising for Committee members. But in some respects, the Committee's interest in allegedly subversive arts people, especially writers such as Miller and Hellman, was a product of the long history of surveillance of American writers by the FBI and other government agencies. HUAC targets often complained about phone taps, being followed, having their mail opened, and so forth. Those complaints were usually dismissed as Communist paranoia, but their truth became clear years later, when FBI and other government records became accessible under the Freedom of Information Act. Writers with significant FBI files included Langston Hughes, Carl Sandburg, Theodore Dreiser, Richard Wright, James Baldwin, Amiri Baraka, Ernest Hemingway, John Steinbeck, and Norman Mailer. Some had been Communists at one point or another. Others simply expressed opinions that

[1] "Red Visitors Cause Rumpus," *Life*, April 4, 1949, pp. 39–43.

struck FBI operatives as "subversive" or "odd" or "un-American." Summaries of FBI surveillance files on writers can be found in Herbert Mitgang's *Dangerous Dossiers* (1988) and in Natalie Robins's *Alien Ink* (1992).[2] Examples of actual surveillance files can currently be found in the "Reading Room" on the FBI website.[3]

While HUAC targeted opinion makers, it also investigated less prominent but still influential people such as teachers, professors, social workers, and mid-level or lower-level government officials. Many of these people were told that they must sign affidavits (i.e., "loyalty oaths") that they were not Communists. Those who refused to sign were usually dismissed and blacklisted.

Beginning in 1949, HUAC published a series of widely distributed pamphlets under the title *100 Things You Should Know About Communism*. These addressed the "Communist conspiracy and its influence in this country as a whole on religion, on education, on labor, and on our government." The pamphlet on education was typical. Set up in question and answer format, its first question was "What is Communism?" The answer: "A conspiracy to conquer and rule the world by any means, legal or illegal." The third question was, "What do the Communists want?" The answer: "To rule your mind and body from the cradle to the grave." Later, the questions became increasingly complex, so that, after noting that many educators had been recruited to the "murderous and destructive cause" of Communism, the 97th question asked, "Are people doing anything about all this?" The answer: "In some places. For instance, Ohio State University faculty members are required to sign the equivalent of non-Communist affidavits. Then, too, in New Jersey, California, Michigan, and Washington State, among others, local authorities have begun investigations of Communist infiltration of schools."

Like other government agencies, HUAC was involved in unmasking those who worked as Soviet spies, and it developed the evidence

---

[2] Herbert Mitgang, *Dangerous Dossiers: Exposing the Secret War Against America's Greatest Authors* (Donald I. Fine, New York, 1988); Natalie Robins, *Alien Ink: The FBI's War on Freedom of Expression* (W. Morrow, New York, 1992).

[3] FBI electronic reading room website is at http://foia.fbi.gov/room.htm

used in the Alger Hiss case, one of the two most famous spy cases of the day. Hiss, whose government career began in 1933, had worked in the high levels of the State Department during and just after World War II and was involved in the planning of the United Nations, serving as secretary general of the UN organizing conference. In 1946, the State Department sought his resignation after being informed by security officials that Hiss had cooperated with Soviet intelligence. In 1947, Hiss was appointed President of the Carnegie Endowment for International Peace. In late 1948, another HUAC witness, Whittaker Chambers, a *Time* magazine editor who had been a CPUSA member in the 1930s, named Hiss as a fellow Communist who had also spied for the Soviet Union.

Hiss denied knowing Chambers, then admitted knowing him but denied supplying the Soviets with confidential State Department information. The dispute played out in public hearings before the Committee, with Chambers producing evidence in Hiss's hand-writing and on Hiss's typewriter and Hiss alleging that he was being framed. The HUAC case was pressed by Congressman Richard Nixon, later the US President. Ultimately, Hiss was convicted of perjury in Federal court because of his HUAC testimony and served three years and eight months of a five-year prison term.

Klaus Fuchs, a physicist who had worked on the Manhattan Project which produced the first atomic bombs, was also convicted of spying for the Soviet Union. But the most widely reported and important spy case of the day was that of Julius and Ethel Rosenberg and a few colleagues. The Rosenbergs and their codefendants were accused by the Department of Justice – HUAC was not directly involved in the case – of participating in a conspiracy to pass secrets on the design and production of the atomic bomb to the Soviet Union.

In July 1950, a few weeks after the beginning of the Korean War, the government indicted members of the alleged spy ring. It alleged that Julius Rosenberg operated the ring, that in 1945 his brother-in-law, David Greenglass, who worked as a draftsman at the atomic bomb project facility in Los Alamos, New Mexico, had stolen secrets for Rosenberg, and that Harry Gold, a courier for Rosenberg, received drawings of a particular atomic bomb element from Greenglass and passed them on to the Soviets in a Jell-o box. During the trial that started in March 1951, Greenglass admitted his involvement, as did his wife Ruth and Gold. The Rosenbergs denied any involvement, maintaining that the whole matter resulted from nothing more than a family dispute. A codefendant, Morton Sobell, also denied his involvement. The Rosenbergs were found guilty, their appeals were denied, and – accompanied by a great deal of protest in the US and other countries – they were executed in June 1953.

From the anti-Communist perspective, the Hiss case illustrated, among other things, that Communists served in government positions in the Roosevelt and Truman administrations, that institutions such as the Carnegie Endowment and the UN were associated with Communism, and that Communists were sometimes suave, urbane graduates of the nation's best universities (Hiss had degrees from Johns Hopkins and Harvard Law). From the same perspective, the Rosenberg case proved the traitorous disloyalty of American Communists and suggested that the Soviets could not have developed their atomic bomb on their own. Since all the Rosenberg defendants were New York Jews, a subtext of the case was the un-Americanness of New York Jews.

From the "anti anti-Communist" perspective (that clumsy term has, however, the virtue of accuracy), the Hiss and Rosenberg cases illustrated how innocent people could be framed, how public opinion could be manipulated by the government, how deeply irrational were the vast majority of citizens who believed the government's lies, and how paranoia and hysteria were at the core of US culture.

In the decades to follow, the Hiss and Rosenberg cases generated a great number of books which, so to speak, reargued the trials. New evidence, such as emerged from Soviet archives after 1989, seemed to many scholars to prove the guilt of both Hiss and Julius Rosenberg, but others found that same evidence to be a continuation of the same old frame-ups. Recently, Morton Sobell, who was convicted with the Rosenbergs and spent 18 years in Federal prisons, and who had always denied his guilt, changed his story. In a *New York Times* article in 2008 it was reported that Sobell was asked again whether he spied.

He was quoting as saying in response, "Yeah, yeah, yeah, call it that. I never thought of it as that in those terms." He also said that Julius Rosenberg had been a spy and that Ethel knew what Julius did but did not participate. He then added that what was given to the Soviets was not valuable information but "junk."[4]

In 1949, as HUAC activities were accelerating and while Communist victories and technological achievements were deepening concern in the West, the Department of Justice began to prosecute leaders of the CPUSA. The legal basis for the prosecutions was the Alien Registration Act of 1940, or Smith Act, which made it a criminal offense

> to knowingly or willfully advocate, abet, advise or teach the duty, necessity, desirability or propriety of overthrowing the Government of the United States or of any State by force or violence, or for anyone to organize any association which teaches, advises or encourages such an overthrow, or for anyone to become a member of or to affiliate with any such association.

At the trial of New York leaders, the first of several Smith Act trials, the defense attorneys argued that the CPUSA was a legal organization that only advocated for its positions, recruited members, and campaigned for election. Its leaders, they said, believed in legal change, electoral politics, and nonviolence. They were decent Americans whose rights to free thought and speech were protected and, more to the point of the prosecution's charges, none had ever committed a "single overt act of force and violence against the Government of the United States" or "ever directly or indirectly advocated its forcible overthrow."

The Smith Act prosecutors declared all of the defense statements to be "mere talk" and "empty phrases" and argued that the leaders were guilty of advocating the violent overthrow of the government because they believed in "Marxism-Leninism," which they defined

[4] Sam Roberts, "Figure in Rosenberg Case Admits to Soviet Spying," *New York Times*, September 11, 2008, p. A1.

as an international conspiracy to create violent revolutions wherever possible. To clarify for jurors what this meant, the prosecutors read aloud lengthy passages from books and pamphlets of Communist political theory and history.

The 11 New York defendants in the first Smith Act trial were found guilty. Ten of them received five-year prison terms and $10,000 fines, one received a three-year prison term. More Smith Act trials of other CP leaders in other cities ensued, so that, ultimately, there were a total of 140 indictments and a total of 93 convictions.

On appeal, the US Supreme Court sustained the first Smith Act convictions, ruling in 1951 that the First Amendment protection of free speech did not apply when the speech posed a "clear and present danger." Then, in 1956, after hearing appeals of post-1951 Smith Act convictions, the Court, under the leadership of the recently appointed Chief Justice Earl Warren, overturned Smith Act convictions, ruling that mere verbal advocacy of revolution was indeed protected free speech.

The Smith Act prosecutions were unconstitutional. But they were nonetheless devastating to the CPUSA because nearly its entire leadership spent years defending themselves in long, expensive, and enervating trials after which they served time in prison or awaited imprisonment. Furthermore, in the eyes of many Americans, Communism had been proven to be a criminal conspiracy.

The HUAC investigations, the Rosenberg case, and the Smith Act trials commanded a great deal of public attention. The investigations and other commotions caused by Senator Joseph McCarthy commanded even more. McCarthy had accused his opponent of Communist sympathies when he had first run for the US Senate in 1946 – in the 1946 elections, this was a standard Republican charge against Democrats – but his career as a prominent anti-Communist on the national stage only began a month after the conviction of Hiss on perjury charges and in the context of the Communist takeover of China.

On February 9, 1950, speaking to a women's group in Wheeling, West Virginia, McCarthy said that Communism was about immorality, that Karl Marx "expelled people from his Communist Party for mentioning such things as love, justice, humanity or morality" and that the US was currently involved in an "all-out battle between Communistic atheism and Christianity." Anti-Communism, then, was not just an effort to contain the Soviets, it was an effort to restore morality that "will end only when the whole sorry mess of twisted, warped thinkers are swept from the national scene so that we have a new birth of honesty and decency in government." Were there immoral Communists in the US government? Of course! And to prove his point, McCarthy said that a piece of paper that he held up had on it "a list of 205" names "that were made known to the Secretary of State as being members of the Communist Party and who nevertheless are still working and shaping policy in the State Department."

Spurred on by the largely positive national news coverage of his Wheeling speech, McCarthy wrote a well-publicized letter to President Truman in which he said that Truman must direct the Secretary of State to dismiss the "57 Communists" (there was nothing said about the 205) who worked in the State Department. "Failure on your part," he told the President, "will label the Democratic Party of being the bedfellow of international communism." The Wheeling accusations and the letter to Truman were the first salvos by McCarthy in what would become four years of charges about Communist infiltration into the Federal government.[5] Because the Democrats controlled the Federal bureaucracy between 1932, when Franklin Roosevelt was elected President, and 1952, when Republican Dwight D. Eisenhower was elected, and because the Democrats controlled the mayoralties and governing bodies in most big cities, the charges obviously were calculated to lead Americans to the conclusion that Democrats were Communist dupes or actual Communists. In this effort, McCarthy was unrestrained. At various times between 1950 and 1952, he said that Truman was "a son-of-a-bitch who ought to be impeached," that the Secretary of Defense, George C. Marshall, was a traitor, and that the Secretary of State, Dean Acheson, was the

---

[5]   McCarthy's Wheeling speech and the letter to Truman are available online at http://historymatters.gmu.edu/d/6456/

"Red Dean." These were just a few of his many loud allegations and denunciations.

After the Republican victories in the 1952 election, McCarthy became the Chairman of the Senate Committee on Government Operations and its Subcommittee on Investigations. These positions permitted him free rein to investigate Communist infiltration of government. To aid him in this effort, he appointed as his Chief Counsel Roy M. Cohn, a brilliant, ruthless, hard-nosed attorney who had been involved in the Rosenberg prosecutions. Through much of 1953, he held well-covered and sometimes televised public hearings on Communist influence in the Foreign Service, the Government Printing Office, the United States Information Service (USIS) overseas libraries run by the State Department, and the Voice of America, which broadcast radio programming aimed at winning the hearts and minds of people in countries where the US was competing with the Soviet Union for influence. No great revelations resulted from those hearings, though it did emerge, for example, that some USIS libraries contained books that had been written by Communists or fellow-travelers and that some Voice of America programming had possibly involved Communists or sympathizers. What also became clear was that McCarthy and Cohn were completely unrestrained: among other things, they aired unsubstantiated charges, bullied witnesses, brought in disgruntled former government employees to testify against their former bosses, and ended hearings abruptly when evidence which did not serve their ends was beginning to emerge. The tactics used against witnesses who were interviewed in private were even more severe, as became evident when the previously secret testimony of some 395 such witnesses was released by the Senate in 2003.

In late 1953 and early 1954, McCarthy moved on to hold hearings on allegations of Communist infiltration of the Signal Corps of the US Army, which was responsible for communications systems and codes. The televised hearings were a disaster for him. Veteran soldiers and officers, including some highly decorated ones, were rudely interrogated about minor and irrelevant details. Scant evidence about the Army "coddling" Communists was produced.

McCarthy and Cohn began to seem as if they had secret agendas that had nothing to do with rooting out Communists. The severely untelegenic McCarthy made wandering speeches. The Army made some telling countercharges about McCarthy's and Cohn's abuse of power.

After 36 days, the Army–McCarthy hearings closed with nothing proven about Communist subversion and with McCarthy himself under investigation by his Senate colleagues. In late 1954, the Senate voted 67–22 to censure McCarthy for bringing the Senate into "dishonor and disrepute."

Despite McCarthy's ignoble end, the anti-Communist cause in America was completely successful by the mid-1950s. The CPUSA had virtually no defenders left and, even if there had been, no newspaper, magazine, publisher, radio program, or television program would have dared to air or print the defense. Moreover, the CPUSA leadership had been eviscerated and its membership was down to a few thousand.

In early 1956, those remaining CPUSA members suffered their greatest trauma ever when they learned that Nikita Khrushchev, the Soviet Premier, had made a "secret speech" to the Twentieth Congress of the Communist Party of the Soviet Union, held in Moscow in February.[6] In that speech, Khrushchev denounced his predecessor, Josef Stalin, who had led the country from 1924 to his death in 1954, for having committed a vast number of criminal acts. Stalin, according to Khrushchev, "practiced brutal violence, not only toward everything which opposed him, but also toward that which seemed to his capricious and despotic character, contrary to his concepts." Stalin, Khrushchev said, demanded "absolute submission" and declared that anyone who disagreed with him was an "enemy of the people" who must be liquidated. He had also ordered "extreme methods and mass repression." People, including many loyal Communist leaders, were forced by brutal torture to confess to crimes that they had not committed and, after "trials" in which

[6]   Khrushchev's "secret speech" is available online at several websites, e.g., http://www.fordham.edu/halsall/mod/krushchev-secret.html

the forced confession was the only evidence, were sentenced to be executed. In addition, Stalin caused the Soviet Union to practice the "cult of the individual," an enforced hero worship under which Stalin was said to be responsible for "all that was good and worthy." Stalin, in short, had been a despotic monster.

By the summer of 1956, a few months after he gave it, Khrushchev's "secret speech" had been widely publicized in Communist countries and in the US press. Its effect on anti-Communists was predictable: they proclaimed that they had all along been on the right side of history, that they had been correct in their estimate of the murderous inhumanity of international Communism and correct about the dangers posed to the nation by the CPUSA and its sympathizers. Its effect on the remaining members of the CPUSA was immediate: many quit in disgust and in shame at having been so duped by propaganda about Stalin's decency and about the Soviet state as a beacon for humankind. Howard Fast, an American who was perhaps the Communist world's most important writer, and who had in 1953 received the Stalin International Peace Prize (a prize set up by the Soviets to compete with the Nobel Peace Prize), spoke for many Communist intellectuals in his *The Naked God*. That short book was unsparing in its denunciation of Soviet Communism's will to murder its real or imagined critics. Fast also spoke about how writers were treated by Communists, saying they were often "emasculated." At its best, literature has always been, Fast said, "searching, impatient, and critical." When Communism prohibits "the critic, the rebel, the prodding, bedeviling, annoying gadfly who disturbs, offends, irritates, and provokes – then you prohibit literature itself."[7]

Anti-Communism did not abate because of Khrushchev's speech. Rather, it continued to play a major role in American domestic politics until 1989, when the Soviet Union dissolved. The containment of Communism continued to be the primary American foreign policy posture. American entrance into the internal affairs of other countries was justified on the basis of the need to halt the spread of

[7] Howard Fast, *The Naked God: The Writer and the Communist Party* (Bodley Head, London, 1958), p. 94.

Communism, to stop Communism here or there so that neighboring countries were prevented from falling in a sort of chain reaction like dominoes. The arms race between the Soviet Union and the US continued. The charge of being "soft on Communism" continued to be heard in electoral campaigns as a way of smearing an opponent.

The Literature

In its heyday, the CPUSA had devoted a good deal of its energy to achieving equality for black Americans. It was therefore of major importance to the Party that the most prominent Depression-era black writer, Richard Wright, was a Communist. And so it was a major event when Wright resigned from the Party and wrote about its shortcomings in an essay titled "I Tried to be a Communist," published in 1944 in the August and September editions of the *Atlantic Monthly*.

At the beginning of his essay, Wright recorded his early 1930s attraction to Communism after he discovered in it "an organized search for the truth of the lives of the oppressed and the isolated," the fact that Communism showed the "similarity of the experiences of workers in other lands," and the possibility of "uniting scattered but kindred peoples into a whole." A few pages later, he turned to what he identified as several serious shortcomings of Communism he had experienced over more than a decade of involvement. Communism, Wright wrote, "missed the meaning of the lives of the masses, had conceived of people in too abstract a manner." Communism changed its positions rapidly and without considera-tion of the people affected, as when the Party announced that the John Reed writers' "clubs," which had attracted Wright and others like him, were to be dissolved. Communists were given to factional-ism and sneaky manipulation, and they believed in having "purges" against members who did not completely support their positions. Each of these shortcomings undercut the standard claims of the CPUSA that it understood the lives and needs of the masses, that it was focused and consistent, and that it was democratic.

The CPUSA always claimed that it deeply respected intellectuals and artists. Wright disagreed. His fellow black Communists, Wright reported, laughed at him because they said he "talks like a book," which, even though he made his living as a Chicago street-cleaner, "was enough to condemn me forever as bourgeois," On one occasion, he was told by a leader that "Intellectuals don't fit well into the Party" and that "The Soviet Union has had to shoot a lot of intellectuals." Wright said that he responded, saying, "You're not in Russia. You're standing on a sidewalk in Chicago. You talk like a man lost in a fantasy." These remarks undercut CPUSA claims regarding its clearheaded understanding of the world. Unwilling to put his beliefs aside, unwilling to simply accept Party dictates on how and what he should think, Wright was labeled a "petty bourgeois degenerate" who was "corrupting the Party," a "bastard intellectual," an "incipient Trotskyite," a person with an "anti-leadership attitude," and a person with "seraphim tendencies," which Wright said meant that he had "withdrawn from the struggle of life and considered [himself] infallible." Ultimately, after Wright made clear that he wanted to leave the Party, he concluded that if the Communists had power, "I should have been declared guilty of treason and my execution would have followed." That last comment, like the leader's comment about how lots of intellectuals had to be shot in the Soviet Union, moved far beyond the other critiques by alleging that Communists were serial murderers. Wright's comments about his CPUSA experience represented a fairly complete endorsement of most of the standard anti-Communist arguments about the true nature of communism.

"I Tried to be a Communist" was reprinted in Richard Crossman's *The God That Failed* (1949), alongside accounts of Communism's shortcomings and terrors by former American, English, and European Communist writers Louis Fischer, Stephen Spender, Arthur Koestler, Ignazio Silone, and André Gide.[8] That book, one of the core documents in the history of international anti-Communism, gave Wright's

[8] Richard Crossman (ed.), *The God That Failed* (Harper, New York, 1949).

essay renewed life just as postwar American anti-Communism was getting into full swing.

Richard Wright left the United States in 1947, taking up permanent residence in Paris. In 1952, he was to return to the US on a visit but ultimately refused to do so because he feared that he would be subpoenaed to testify by HUAC. His fears were no doubt justified, for he would have been seen by the Committee as a potential treasure trove of names.

Another prominent black writer, Langston Hughes, did not manage to avoid publicly testifying about his past involvement with Communism. Subpoenaed by Senator McCarthy in March 1953 regarding the placement of 16 of his books in USIS libraries in other countries in a program aimed at "propagandizing our way of life and our system," Hughes testified in executive session and then, a few days later, in public in a televised session. In the executive session, he first claimed that he "had never been a believer in communism or a Communist party member" but, pressed hard by Roy Cohn and warned of the penalties for perjury, he then said that as a non-Communist he had once desired the Soviet form of government for the US but with "many modifications." Asked about poems that seemed to Cohn to clearly endorse communism, such as "Goodbye, Christ," Hughes maintained that readers may have misinterpreted him because "poetry may mean many things to many people." The transcript of these executive session comments did not become public until 2003, when the Senate Permanent Subcommittee on Investigations released them in print and online.[9]

Some arrangement must have been made between Hughes, his attorney, and Senator McCarthy after the executive session, because when Hughes appeared in the March 24, 1953 public session he was said to be a "cooperating witness." In his testimony, Hughes declared that around 1950 he had changed his mind about Communism and democracy because he now recognized the "lack of freedom of expression in the Soviet Union for writers," because there had been

---

[9]   See   http://www.senate.gov/artandhistory/history/resources/pdf/Volume2.pdf for Hughes's testimony at the executive session.

significant "improvement in race relations" in the US, and because
he had read reports about the treatment of minorities in the USSR,
some of which indicated "persecution and terror against the Jewish
people."

Like Wright's 1944 essay, Hughes's testimony directly undercut
CPUSA claims about the benevolent treatment of minorities in the
Soviet Union, saying, in effect, that the Soviet system held no hopes
for blacks and other minorities, while the US was beginning to treat
its minorities better. This was an extremely important statement by
a world class black writer that came at just that moment when the
US and the Soviets were embroiled in a fierce competition for the
allegiance of Africans and other colonized people who were throwing
off their colonial masters. Who better to speak on the merits of the
two systems than a disaffected black American who had at one time
been attracted by Communism but had now come to his senses?
Hughes's statement, like Wright's, had geopolitical as well as domestic applications.

After extracting those comments about his change of mind, Roy
Cohn turned over the examination of Hughes to Senator McCarthy,
who wanted to know whether Hughes thought that the 16 books of
his that had been purchased for the USIS libraries followed the
"Communist line." Hughes responded that "Some of these books
very largely followed at times some aspects of the Communist line,
reflecting my sympathy with them. But not all of them, sir." McCarthy
then asked, "Do you feel that those books should be on our shelves
throughout the world, with the apparent stamp of approval of the
United States government?" Hughes responded with, "I was certainly
amazed to hear that they were. I was surprised, and I would certainly
say 'No.'"[10]

That comment by Hughes represented a victory for McCarthy,
who had been arguing for censorship of the contents of USIS
libraries. Some of his opponents had been maintaining that the
country could not advertise its freedom and liberty to overseas

[10] See http://www.archive.org/stream/statedepartmenti01unit/
statedepartmenti01unit_djvu.txt

audiences by suppressing the content of libraries, while others argued that the label "Communist" was too loosely applied by people like McCarthy. Hughes's remark about his amazement that the government would use his 16 books settled the debate; it must have seemed to McCarthy and other anti-Communists that the USIS officials who chose the books were more red than Hughes himself. Newspaper accounts of Hughes's testimony followed that line and also simplified it. On March 27, the *New York Times* published an article about the writer Dashiell Hammett's appearance at the inquiry. After commenting on Hammett's refusal to cooperate, the *Times* reporter summarized the testimony by Hughes and the similar testimony by writer Edwin Seaver by saying that "both said that if they were fighting communism they would not have selected their books for a government information program."[11]

A great and influential novel, Ralph Ellison's *Invisible Man* (1952) was celebrated in the 1950s and beyond as a beautifully crafted, penetrating analysis of black identity and an astute commentary on the dangers posed to individual freedom by institutions and organizations. Set mostly in the mid-1930s, it carries its unnamed first person narrator from childhood in the Jim Crow South, through a couple of years of education at a black southern college that had little connection to the lives of the black southern masses, to Harlem and downtown Manhattan where he became a featured speaker for an organization called the Brotherhood, and from there to a surreal, isolated underground place just outside Harlem. More than half of the novel is focused on the Brotherhood experience.

Invisible Man contains an account of the Brotherhood's ideology and a detailed picture of its activities in Harlem in the 1930s. According to the Brotherhood, it had a purely scientific approach to the world, and it was able to say what was "correct" and what was "incorrect" in all circumstances. Its ideology can explain all phenomena; as the narrator himself reports, "Nothing lay outside the scheme

[11] C. P. Trussell, "Dashiell Hammett Silent at Inquiry," *New York Times*, March 27, 1953, p. 9.

of our ideology, there was a policy on everything. ..." Beyond science, the Brotherhood believes in historical certainty, and so there are many remarks made about history having passed some people by, the unity of opposites that underlies all history, the claim that the Brothers will move history forward, and so forth. Beyond scientism and historical determinism, Ellison's Brotherhood claims that it understands the "people" as no other organization does, that their program for change will restore to the "people" the "heritage" that has been taken from them, and that ultimately there will be a non-racial "Rainbow of America's Future," as one of its banners says. Other details about the beliefs of the Brotherhood include its rejection of race as a social determinant, its interest in promoting inter-racial relationships, its promotion of "folk" music composed by Party people who were not the folk, and its loosening of sexual strictures. From leaders like the Invisible Man, who becomes Chief Spokesman for the Harlem District, the Party demands complete and total submission to its discipline, including the submersion of personal ambitions, the putting aside of prior education, the submission to reeducation through "indoctrination," the adoption of a new name, and the ending of relationships with family and friends. Each of Ellison's details – and many others I have not listed – expresses almost exactly the ideology of the actual CPUSA.

Ellison reveals all of the Brotherhood's beliefs and behaviors to be illusory or worse. It is hopelessly out of touch with the masses it wishes to liberate, its ideology is rigid and impractical, it is hypocritical, it is beset by bureaucratic infighting, and it is racist even as it proclaims its love of black people. Stated at the end of the novel's "Prologue," the unnamed narrator's conclusion about his experience with the "Brotherhood" is clear: the period of his life when he was involved with it was "sad" and "lost."

That every one of the characteristics and beliefs of the Brotherhood was a core characteristic of the CPUSA was noticed by Communist reviewers of *Invisible Man*, who saw the book as an attack on the Party. A review in the *Daily Worker* said that "Ellison's work manipulates his nameless hero for 439 pages through a maze of corruption, brutality, anti-communism slanders, sex perversion and the sundry inhumanities upon which a dying system feeds."[12] In the June 1952 issue of the Communist magazine *Masses and Mainstream*, Lloyd Brown said that he would not "attempt to refute the particular variations of the antiCommunist lie that Ellison tells." Instead, he pointed to reviews in the anti-Communist press that indicated that even the most extreme anti-Communists thought that Ellison had gone too far:

> Some idea of his writing on this subject can be gained when we see even the *New Leader*, second to none in Redbaiting viciousness, complaining that "Ellison's Communists are hard to believe, they are so unrelievedly humorless, cynical and degenerate (including the black Communists)." And the *Nation*'s reviewer, who says he is "ready to believe" the worst about "Harlem Stalinists" grumbles: "The trouble with such caricature is that it undermines the intention behind it." (Nevertheless he finds the book "exalted.").[13]

Despite the fact that the Brotherhood's core beliefs duplicated those of the CPUSA, Ellison said in interviews at the time of the publication of *Invisible Man*, then when he won the National Book Award for it, and in later interviews, that his Brotherhood had nothing to do with the CPUSA. Usually, he couched the denial in the assertion that he was a nonpolitical writer because, as an artist deeply influenced by T. S. Eliot and other Modernists, he understood that politics and literature did not mix well. Literary critics and teachers of literature who subscribed to postwar critical theories that great literature was never political applauded Ellison's position and discussed *Invisible Man* as one of the great Modernist texts that explored and finally endorsed the lonely journey of the individual in a world full of people and institutions assailing his selfhood. So far as I know, other than the Communist press reviewers I already

---

[12]   Abner N. Berry, "Ralph Ellison's Novel 'Invisible Man' Shows Snobbery, Contempt for Negro People," *Daily Worker*, June 1, 1952, section 2, p. 7.
[13]   Lloyd L. Brown, "The Deep Pit," *Masses and Mainstream*, 5, no. 6 (June, 1952), pp. 62–4.

mentioned, no early commentators ever thought of *Invisible Man* as an anti-Communist text or even as a Modernist text with anti-Communist elements.

Ellison's story about his apolitical outlook went unchallenged for several decades. Finally, Thomas Hill Schaub, drawing partly on Ellison's 1930s publications, wrote about some of the political aspects of *Invisible Man* in *American Fiction in the Cold War* (1991). Several years later, Barbara Foley argued that anti-Communism was a central issue in the novel and that during the later 1930s Ellison "vigorously endorsed and supported the program and outlook of the U. S. Communist left." Foley based her commentary on a full reading of all three dozen pieces of work Ellison published in 1930s left-wing magazines such as *New Challenge, New Masses, Direction, Tomorrow, Negro Quarterly, and Negro Story*. She concluded that "Ellison's partisans were clearly willing to expunge a resume indicating high productivity in order to guarantee him acceptable writerly credentials. The 'Ralph Ellison' packaged for Cold War public consumption was, to borrow a phrase from William Carlos Williams, a pure product of America."[14] In his 2007 biography of Ellison, Arnold Rampersad provided many further details about the writer's involvement with Communists and the CPUSA in the 1930s, his extensive reading of Marx, his closeness to Richard Wright, his attendance at CPUSA writers' conferences, and his deep interest in "the welfare of the Party and the anti-Fascist cause." Interestingly, regarding Communist attacks on *Invisible Man* such as I have already quoted, Rampersad cites a manuscript letter written by Ellison to Richard Wright in which Ellison said that they "only made members desire to read the book" and that he knew, in Rampersad's words, that those attacks "made him exempt from being called a Communist, much less a Communist sympathizer."[15] By 1943, according to Rampersad,

---

[14] Barbara Foley, "Ralph Ellison as Proletarian Journalist," *Science and Society*, 62, no. 4 (Winter 1998–99), pp. 537–56.

[15] Arnold Rampersad, *Ralph Ellison: A Biography* (Alfred A. Knopf, New York, 2007), p. 262 .

Ellison had withdrawn from his commitment to the CPUSA ("if he had ever been a member," he adds).[16]

What did Ellison have to fear if he had simply acknowledged his Communist past and explained it as a "youthful indiscretion," the "mistake" of a young man, and pointed to his treatment of the Brotherhood as persuasive evidence of his change of mind and heart? My answer to that question has two parts. First, 1952 was one of the crests in the history of American anti-Communism and that meant, among other things, that writing by Communists or former Communists was simply not issued by major publishers. Second, had he admitted his past associations, Ellison would soon have been subjected to a HUAC investigation (and perhaps a McCarthy investigation, too) that would have tested the sincerity of his anti-Communism by requiring him to name his former Communist comrades and to provide other information.

Anti-communism infused American popular entertainment in the postwar era. Directly and indirectly, comic books, magazines, romance novels, adventure novels and the like expressed the values of anti-Communism and the glorious deeds of righteous, freedom-loving heroes. Great numbers of anti-communist films – for example, *I Married a Communist* (1949), *The Red Menace* (1949), *I Was a Communist for the FBI* (1951), *Atomic City* (1952), *Trial* (1955), *Rio Bravo* (1956), and *Silk Stockings* (1957) – were produced by Hollywood studios. In addition, a number of science fiction films, such as *Invaders from Mars* (1953), *Them* (1954), and *Invasion of the Body Snatchers* (1956), were commonly interpreted to be anti-Communist cautionary tales.

Did *Invisible Man* fit the mold of those popular anti-Communist entertainments? I do not think so – Ellison's craft and his often magical command of language and his brilliant range put him in a class of his own. Did *Invisible Man* serve the anti-Communist cause by teaching countless numbers of readers across generations about the nature and hopelessness of Communism even if they were misled by its author and his scholars into believing that the Brotherhood

[16]   Rampersad (2007), p. 162.

was not the CPUSA and that Ellison himself had always been an apolitical artist? Along with Wright's renunciation of Communism and McCarthy's taming of Langston Hughes, did it add to the world's understanding that the most important black American intellectuals found Communism inadequate and hypocritical? Did it help to move those who sought equality for black Americans away from the CPUSA? Absolutely.

But here is a qualification about the alienation of black American intellectuals from Communism. W. E. B. DuBois, the greatest and most enduring of them, became more and more involved with Communism in the postwar years and even became an unofficial apologist for Stalin's methods by arguing that they were caused by the constant US efforts to subvert the Soviet state. In 1961, in his nineties, as he was preparing to move permanently to Ghana, DuBois joined the CPUSA.

Boom Times

During the four years the United States was engaged in World War II, its industrial production more than doubled. In 1945, the US was the world's only large industrial nation whose economy had not been severely damaged or completely destroyed in World War II and by 1947 it produced about half of the world's manufactured goods. Until other countries rebuilt their economies, which in most cases took two decades or more, US companies had almost no competitors in overseas markets.

The immediate postwar years were just the beginning of economic good times. From 1945 to the early 1970s, the US production of goods and services doubled. Between 1941 and 1969, family income nearly doubled and the standard of living, even among working-class Americans, surged. Living standards, and national well-being, too, were typically measured by home and car ownership. During the Depression and the war, the home construction industry came to a virtual standstill; after the war, construction boomed, and by 1960 three out of five families owned their own home. During the Depression, auto production had slowed and during the war it had ceased almost entirely; after the war, auto production boomed (five million new cars were sold in 1949, for example) and by 1970 there were two cars on American roads for every three adults. Higher living standards and the rapidly increasing output of goods and services were accompanied by or led to high birth rates, significant increases in college enrollments, increasing consumer spending, spreading access to television and the expansion of television coverage of news, sports, and entertainment, the spread of shopping malls across much of the country, the construction of an extensive interstate highway system, the increasing use of credit cards, and increasing levels of both domestic and international tourism. During the 1950s, the fast food industry boomed, as did the modern motel industry and discount retail stores. Even the Cold War and the threats posed by international Communism, as well as the Korean War and the Vietnam War, were good for the American economy: military spending was an economic pillar throughout the period.

All of this expansion took place in a period when inflation remained low and when unemployment, even during recessions, stayed below 5 percent. The low unemployment figures – less than 5 percent was said to be "full" employment – were helped by continuing low immigration through the 1960s.

Unionization took hold in the 1950s as it never had previously: by 1953, 35 percent of the workforce was unionized. In the core industrial region of the country, an area extending roughly from Boston to Baltimore and across into the upper Midwest, unionized work prevailed in the manufacturing sector. That translated into high wages and, increasingly, fringe benefits such as medical insurance, paid vacations, and pension plans. The period is now sometimes referred to as the "golden age" of American capitalism. It was also the golden age for unions in terms of membership, which translated into sharp increases in revenues generated by dues and, as a result, sharp increases in the power of unions to influence politicians, to negotiate contracts from positions of power, and to conduct strikes and other job actions.

The general sense that in the 1950s the US became something that the world had never seen before, a society characterized by never-ending and sustainable abundance, was captured in the title of Professor David Potter's *People of Plenty* (1954). Potter did not simply comment on all the indications of abundance. Regarding social mobility, the basis of the all-important concept of equality of opportunity, Potter wrote that "America has had a greater measure of social equality and social mobility than any highly developed society in human history" and that "At every stage, the channels of mobility have been kept open." Regarding "social distinctions," he wrote that "certainly they exist; but, whatever their power may be, social rank can seldom assert an open claim to deference in this country, and it usually makes at least a pretense of conformity to equalitarian ways. Certain conspicuous exceptions, such as the treatment of American Negroes, qualify all these assertions but do not invalidate them as generalizations."[17] Professor Potter was not just speaking for himself but, rather, was speaking for many academics, politicians, and other movers and shakers; and *People of Plenty* soon became a book used by the government in its United States Information Agency libraries around the world to inform foreign intellectuals and students about the American achievement.

On July 24, 1959, at a trade show in Moscow called the American National Exhibition, Vice President Richard M. Nixon met in a model suburban house with the Premier of the

---

[17] David M. Potter, *People of Plenty: Economic Abundance and the American Character* (University of Chicago Press, 1954), pp. 95–6.

Soviet Union, Nikita S. Khrushchev. In an impromptu discussion, they debated with good humor the merits of the Communist and capitalist systems. Their debate was captured by television crews and later broadcast. I have reproduced here part of the text, because the dialogue sharply conveyed the sense of achievement and confidence of Vice President Nixon as well as the attitudes of Premier Khrushchev:

NIXON: This house can be bought for $14,000, and most Americans can buy a home in the bracket of $10,000 to $15,000. Let me give you an example that you can appreciate. Our steel workers as you know, are now on strike. But any steel worker could buy this house. They earn $3 an hour. This house costs about $100 a month to buy on a contract running 25 to 30 years.

KHRUSHCHEV: We have steel workers and peasants who can afford to spend $14,000 for a house. Your American houses are built to last only 20 years so builders could sell new houses at the end. We build firmly. We build for our children and grandchildren.

NIXON: American houses last for more than 20 years, but, even so, after 20 years, many Americans want a new house or a new kitchen. Their kitchen is obsolete by that time ….The American system is designed to take advantage of new inventions and new techniques.

KHRUSHCHEV: This theory does not hold water. Some things never get out of date – houses, for instance, and furniture, furnishings perhaps but not houses. I have read much about America and American houses, and I do not think that this exhibit and what you say is strictly accurate.

NIXON: Well, um …

KHRUSHCHEV: I hope I have not insulted you.

NIXON: I have been insulted by experts. Everything we say is in good humor. Always speak frankly.

KHRUSHCHEV: The Americans have created their own image of the Soviet man. But he is not as you think. You think the

Russian people will be dumbfounded to see these things, but the fact is that newly built Russian houses have all this equipment right now.

NIXON: Yes, but ...

KHRUSHCHEV: In Russia, all you have to do to get a house is to be born in the Soviet Union. You are entitled to housing ... In America, if you don't have a dollar you have a right to choose between sleeping in a house or on the pavement. Yet you say we are the slave to Communism.

Earlier in the same month, July 1959, that Vice President Nixon debated Premier Khrushchev in that model middle-class suburban house with that up-to-date kitchen, the young socialist writer Michael Harrington published in *Commentary* magazine an article titled "Our Fifty Million Poor." Using published, commonplace United States government data, Harrington pointed out that about one-third of the nation lived below the poverty line that the government itself defined. These Americans, according to Harrington, existed in a "culture of poverty," a "separate culture, another nation, with its own way of life." Most lived in places – city slums and rural areas such as Appalachia – that middle-class people never saw. They were thus "invisible" to their fellow Americans and, obviously, powerless.[18] A year and a half later, the rural poor became somewhat more visible to Americans. On November 26, 1960, the day after Thanksgiving, the major television show *CBS Reports* aired a special, titled "Harvest of Shame," on the circumstances of East Coast migrant agricultural workers. The program opened with the narrator, Edward R. Murrow, commenting on a group of workers gathering at the beginning of what they hoped would be a day of work. Murrow said:

---

[18] Michael Harrington, "Our Fifty Million Poor: Forgotten Men of the Affluent Society," *Commentary* 28, no. 1 (July 1959), pp. 19–27.

> This scene is not taking place in the Congo. It has nothing to
> do with Johannesburg or Cape Town. It is not Nyasaland or
> Nigeria. This is Florida. These are citizens of the United
> States, 1960. This is a shape-up for migrant workers. The
> hawkers are chanting the going piece rate at the various
> fields. This is the way the humans who harvest the food for
> the best-fed people in the world get hired. One farmer
> looked at this and said, "We used to own our slaves; now we
> just rent them."

Many of the images and stories that viewers were given in the
next hour were horrifying.

In 1962, Harrington added more details to his analysis in
The Other America, a book whose main points was not seriously challenged and that was read favorably within the
Kennedy administration. In 1965, in his Inaugural Address to
the nation, President Lyndon Johnson proclaimed an "uncon-
ditional war on poverty" to be waged by his administration.
Before long, the notion that all Americans lived in a plentiful
world, that all shared in the fruits of capitalism, was dismissed
and forgotten. Through the 1960s and beyond, a great deal of
social science research, investigative journalism, and government reports documented poverty amidst plenty, fundamental
inequalities based on race and class in particular.

3

Bad and Mad

The Context

In the 1950s and 1960s, there was some triumphalism expressed in the US, some assertiveness about how the country was the best that had ever existed in the world, the number one place in God's universe. But there were also assertions about the "sickness" of American society. The "rat race" of making money and more money to buy more and more useless things made people crazy, it was said, by defining them down to robotic consumers with no inner lives. There were also suggestions that people were made crazy by remembering the mass deaths of World War II, by paranoia about Communism, and by the understanding that at any moment the whole world could be incinerated by nuclear bombs as a result of the Soviet–US arms race. Most often, though, commentators on societal "sickness" were less grandiose and more focused on mundane problems that they understood to be incrementally toxic and destructive.

As soon as World War II ended, there was considerable expression of public concern about the lack of available housing for returning veterans, unemployment, high divorce rates, juvenile delinquency, and mental illness. The housing shortage was a direct result of the fact that there had been little new construction for many years, and within a couple of years it began to abate as the construction industry boomed in American suburbs. The unemployment problem was soon settled as the country entered its period of tremendous economic expansion. The high divorce rate, usually explained as a consequence of quick and poorly planned wartime marriages or the result of couples drifting away from each other because of long wartime separations, abated after 1947. The other two public concerns, juvenile delinquency and mental illness, continued to trouble the society for many years following the war. On occasion the two were linked, but more often they were seen as two major but separate symptoms of what were said to be the country's deep-seated social ills.

Juvenile delinquency – that is, offenses against the law by people less than 18 years of age – had long been recognized as a problem. But, judging by newspaper and magazine coverage, it became the country's *most* discussed postwar subject. Even as the war was ending in 1945, there were widespread news stories of teenagers involved in gang wars, street fights, and murders as well as lesser offenses like shoplifting and vandalism. In the one month before the atomic bombings of Hiroshima and Nagasaki and in the one month afterwards, the *New York Times* – not a sensationalist publication – published several such stories.[1] In the 16 months between the end of the war and the beginning of 1947, the weekly *New York Times Magazine* published eight articles on the subject of juvenile delinquency. Other weekly and monthly magazines aimed at general audiences also featured it.[2] On some days, tabloid newspapers in major cities seemed *only* to feature stories about delinquents and their outrages.

A 1946 article in the *New York Times* attempted to summarize current trends. "Our great year of victory abroad, 1945, was a year of defeat on one of the most vital sectors of the home front," the

[1]   These *New York Times* articles included "17 Boys Arrested in Fatal Gang Riot," July 21, 1945, p. 13, which was about two rival black gangs in Brooklyn's Bedford-Stuyvesant neighborhood; "2 Fighting Boys Fall From Movie Balcony," August 2, 1945, p. 8; "Boy, 10, Fatally Shot; Playmate, 12, Arrested by the Police in Yonkers Tragedy," August 13, 1945, p. 21; "40 Negro Youths Disrupt V-J Block Party With Knives and Bottles – 14 Are Arrested," September 3, 1945, p. 25.

[2]   Stories that came out in 1946 included "The Children's Hour," *Time*, XLVII, no. 2 (January 14, 1946); "Atlanta's Junior Hoodlums," *Newsweek*, April 1, 1946; "War's Insecurity Lifts Youthful Crime 100%," *Life*, 20 (April 8, 1946), pp. 83–93; Charles J. Dutton, "Tomorrow's Gangsters," *Reader's Digest*, 49, no. 291 (July 1946); and "What Juvenile Crime Reflects," *Ladies' Home Journal*, October 1946.

story began. It then went on to report that FBI statistics indicated that in 1945 crime in 2,000 cities had increased by 12.4 percent and, even more shocking, that 20 percent of people arrested were minors, that the average age of the American criminal was now 17. The story also pointed out that, according to President Truman, some categories of juvenile crime had increased 350 percent since Pearl Harbor, and it called for concerted action by government at all levels. It ended with a reiteration of the conventional explanation of the causes of the epidemic: children were not given proper discipline and the authority of institutions such as the home, the church, the school, and the law had become too "relaxed."[3]

Two months later the *New York Times* reported on the stance taken by US Attorney General Tom C. Clark.[4] As in most public assessments of the causes of delinquency, the comments by law enforcement officials quoted in the article stressed the breakdown of family life and parents who shirked responsibility as the fundamental causes of the juvenile crime wave.

As some readers must have already noticed, this sense that juvenile delinquency posed a profound challenge to the postwar nation was articulated just weeks after the recognition that Communism was a grave threat; the *Times*'s article on the "Rise of Juvenile Crime" was published just a few weeks after Winston Churchill's comments on the iron curtain and George Kennan's comments on containment.[5]

Widespread discussions of juvenile delinquency and news reports of sensational crimes committed by the young continued through the 1950s. Even the US Senate expressed its interest and concern. The Senate Subcommittee to Investigate Juvenile Delinquency in the United States held sessions from 1954 to 1956, most famously declaring that the consumption of violent comic books by juveniles was the major cause of their criminal behavior. Every year saw the publication of at least several hundred newspaper and magazine articles

---

[3] "Rise of Juvenile Crime," *New York Times*, March 21, 1946, p. 24.
[4] "Clark Fears Era of Lawless Youth: Attorney General Warns Every Community Must Accept Its Responsibility to Nation," *New York Times*, May 12, 1946, p. 15.
[5] See Chapter 2, pp. 28, 29.

as well as countless news items reporting on particular crimes and outrages. Some major Hollywood films closely or somewhat more loosely focused on the topic, including *The Wild One* (1954), *Blackboard Jungle* (1955), and *Rebel Without a Cause* (1955). Dozens of other films also appeared; releases in 1959, for example, included *The Beat Generation, The Bloody Brood, Cry Tough, Daddy-O, Girls Town, High School Confidential, The Rebel Set, Riot in Juvenile Prison, Serious Charge,* and *T-Bird Gang.* One of the great Broadway musicals, *West Side Story*, which told the story of the clash of two New York Street gangs, was made into a movie in 1961.

Social scientists, law enforcement officials, and journalists saw juvenile delinquency as deviant, antisocial, criminal activity. Some of the movies I have mentioned, on the other hand, suggested that juvenile delinquents were more interesting and complex, as well as more entertaining, than officials and journalists usually allowed. This was obviously the case with Marlon Brando's character in *The Wild One* and James Dean's character in *Rebel Without a Cause*, and with some of the "beatnik" characters in *The Beat Generation, The Bloody Brood, High School Confidential,* and *The Rebel Set.* In many if not all of these cases, what society called delinquency, or even mature criminality, was reimagined as brooding and righteous rebellion against, variously, the crass stupidity of parents, teachers, and other authorities; the oppressive social order; the miserable world that was being passed on to the young by crazed adults; the emptiness and meaninglessness of middle-class life, and so forth. Many also posed fundamental questions about whether sullen, rebellious, destructive but sometimes sensitive, misunderstood juveniles and young men could be rescued and made into solid citizens.

The most popular and influential book of the postwar era which argued that deviants were righteous rebels was Paul Goodman's *Growing Up Absurd* (1960). Goodman was not naïve. He recognized that deviant boys and young men made choices and invented ways of living that were "rarely charming, usually stupid, and often disastrous," which was not much better than the "for the most part apathetic, disappointed, cynical, and wasted" behavior of "conforming" young men. But he was unrelenting and sometimes brilliant in arguing that there were profound social causes for deviant behavior. Because thoughts similar to Goodman's underlay so much of the literature of youthful rebellion, I will quote him at some length:

> Our abundant society is at present simply deficient in many of the most elementary objective opportunities and worth-while goals that could make growing up possible. It is lacking in enough man's work. It is lacking in honest public speech, and people are not taken seriously. It is lacking in the opportunity to be useful. It thwarts aptitude and creates stupidity. It corrupts ingenuous patriotism. It corrupts the fine arts. It shackles science. It dampens animal ardor. It discourages the religious convictions of Justification and Vocation. It dims the sense that there is a Creation. It has no Honor. It has no Community.

At the end of this litany, Goodman said, "I have nothing novel to say in this book; these are the things that *everybody* knows."[6]

Like discussions of juvenile delinquency, discussions of mental illness were more widespread in the postwar era than they had been in any prior period. Like those about juvenile delinquency, articles about mental illness began to appear in the press shortly after the war ended and continued intensively into the 1960s. Three types of articles dominated. One type reported on murders and other crimes committed by mentally ill individuals, a second reported on efforts to document how many seriously mentally ill people there were in the US and on subgroups in which mental illness was especially prevalent, and a third reported on the chronically ill-equipped, underfunded, and understaffed American mental health care system.

Articles about crimes committed by the mentally ill ran constantly in the more sensationalist press. In many instances, the subtext of these stories was that people who became suddenly insane were quite ordinary family members and neighbors. Occasionally, a story about the "nice man who went criminally insane" was big enough or sensational enough to merit national attention. This was the case with

---

[6] Paul Goodman, *Growing Up Absurd* (Random House, New York, 1960), pp. 12, 13.

one Howard B. Unruh, a New Jersey man whose quick transition from "mild, soft-spoken" veteran of many artillery battles to crazed murderer ran in the *New York Times* in September 1949.[7]

Press reports of people going rapidly insane were common enough in, say, 1930 or even 1830, and the fact that mental illness was a serious contemporary problem was generally recognized during World War II, when some 12 percent of draftees, almost two million men, were rejected because they had "neuropsychiatric" conditions that made them unfit for duty. But postwar reports of great numbers of Americans as well as people in other countries who suffered from serious mental illness were constant and shocking. In 1948, there was an International Congress on Mental Health convened in London, with 37 nations in attendance. At that Congress, the US Surgeon General reported that "one-seventeenth of the nation is psychotic, either confined in institutions or belonging in them" and that one out of every ten people then alive in the country would spend some part of his or her life in a mental institution. This fact was reported in a July 1948 *New York Times* article.[8] The psychotic "one-seventeenth" of the nation was about eight million people. By 1955, according to the US Secretary of Health, as reported in the *New York Times*, the number was nine million, about six percent of the population.[9] Similar articles appeared in magazines such as *Newsweek*. For instance, a January 1947 *Newsweek* story reported that some 840,000 preschool and school-age children suffered from "neurotic behavior problems" and that each year about 1,000 children under age 15 were sent to institutions for the insane; a January 1948 story reported that half the hospital beds in the nation were occupied by "victims of mental disease"; and a March 1955 article

---

[7] Meyer Berger, "Veteran Kills 12 in Mad Rampage on Camden Street: Shoots 4 Others in Revenge for 'Derogatory Remarks' About His Character." *New York Times*, September 7, 1949, p. 1.

[8] Lucy Freeman, "World Fight Near on Mental Illness," *New York Times*, July 19, 1948, p. 21.

[9] Bess Furman, "Program Pushed For Mental Ills," *New York Times*, March 9, 1955, p. 22.

reported that one in twelve children would spend time in mental institutions.[10]

The treatment of mental disorders was in its infancy in the 1950s. Psychotherapy, which at the time usually meant Freudian therapy and involved costly talks over many months or years between patient and therapist, was available but not to the masses of sufferers. Electroconvulsive therapy, known to laypeople as "shock therapy," was widely used (and still is) to treat "mood" and other disorders by sending electrical current through the brain, thereby stimulating it. General anesthetics began to be used with the procedure in the late 1950s, lessening the severity of side effects. Prefrontal lobotomy, the most infamous of treatments, involved the surgical scraping of the cerebral cortex. Beginning in the late 1940s, in what was intended to be a method that could be used rapidly in public hospitals for mentally ill patients, the nerve fibers connecting the cerebral cortex and the thalamus were severed by inserting an instrument through the upper eyelid of a patient. The procedure, banned in several countries in the 1950s but used in the US into the 1970s, often but not always resulted in the complete destruction of personality but usually made patients easier to manage (only killing them outright would have made them more manageable, according to critics). Pharmacological treatments, that is, the use of prescribed drugs to treat mental disorders, began with the development of chlorpromazine in 1952 and its later marketing in the US as Thorazine. By the mid-1950s, there were reports of clinical trials that indicated that the synthetic compound had dramatic "tranquilizing" effects on patients. In one of the earliest public reports, the *New York Times* in a June 1955 article remarked that investigators thought new drugs would "revolutionize" the care of patients suffering from psychoses, neuroses, and anxiety.[11]

[10] "Sick Young Minds," *Newsweek*, January 20, 1947; "American Madhouse," *Newsweek*, January 12, 1948; "Mental Health: One Child in Twelve," *Newsweek*, March 14, 1955.

[11] Howard A. Rusk, "Aid for the Mentally Ill; A Report on the Effectiveness of Two New Drugs in Treating Certain Cases," *New York Times*, June 26, 1955, p. 49.

The low quality of care that was available to people with mental illness was recognized as a major social problem. As many newspaper and magazine articles noted, public hospital facilities for mentally ill patients were notoriously overcrowded and understaffed and these facilities were, in fact, more like warehouses than hospitals. Resident psychiatrists had enormous caseloads that prevented them from doing any in-depth work with patients. Nursing staffs were usually stretched thin, also. The result, too often, was scandalously inhumane treatment of mentally ill patients.

A 1948 book, Albert Deutsch's *The Shame of the States*, was the earliest extended postwar investigation of the public treatment facilities available. Deutsch was a prominent, respected social historian and investigative journalist best known among doctors and psychiatrists for his then-definitive *The Mentally Ill in America* (1937). *The Shame of the States*, which echoed the title *The Shame of the Cities*, Lincoln Steffens's 1904 account of municipal corruption, described the conditions which existed in the 190 state hospitals for mentally ill patients in the US. Separate chapters were devoted to some of the worst, including hospitals in Philadelphia, Cleveland, Detroit, New York, California's Napa Valley, and Milledgeville, Georgia. Deutsch had full access to the hospitals and visited many. As he passed through the wards of the Philadelphia State Hospital for Mental Diseases, known as Byberry, he wrote that he was

> reminded of the pictures of the Nazi concentration camps at Belsen and Buchenwald. I entered buildings swarming with naked humans herded like cattle and treated with less concern, pervaded by a fetid odor so heavy, so nauseating, that the stench seemed to have almost a physical existence of its own. I saw hundreds of patients living under leaking roofs, surrounded by moldy, decaying walls, and sprawling on rotting floors for want of seats and benches.[12]

If any readers thought Deutsch was exaggerating, they had merely to look at the accompanying photograph of the "incontinent ward,"

[12] Albert Deutsch, *The Shame of the States* (Harcourt Brace, New York, 1948), p. 42.

crammed with men standing and lying in their own excreta. At the Napa Valley hospital, a newspaperman who accompanied Deutsch on his tour remarked, "some of the things here are tougher on the guts than watching our men fight and die in the Pacific."[13]

Neglect was the result of overcrowding and underfunding. Byberry was typical. Built for 3,400 patients, it had 6,100. By professional standards, there should have been 1,100 attendants, but there were only 180; there should have been 200 nurses, but there were only 41; and there should have been 34 physicians but there were only 14. Like nearly all the other state hospitals, Deutsch concluded, it was an inhumane warehouse. Moreover, at Byberry and other hospitals, patients were sometimes punished by attendants who sadistically abused them. The shameful conditions of the mental institutions finally led Deutsch, in a chapter titled "Euthanasia Through Neglect," to raise questions about the nature of American civilization. "We are not like the Nazis," he wrote, "We do not kill off 'insane' people coldly as a matter of official state policy. We do not kill them deliberately. We do it by neglect."[14] Later, he asked, "How civilized are we, really? Is a culture which, by inaction, condones the death of sick innocents through neglect significantly purer, in terms of public morals, than a society which sanctions their outright murder by lethal instruments?"[15]

Postwar movies about or involving mental illness, like those about juvenile delinquency, played to and deepened public interest and understanding. The more important ones, some of which became film classics, were *Spellbound* (1945), *The Snake Pit* (1948), *A Streetcar Named Desire* (1951), *Three Faces of Eve* (1957), *Psycho* (1960), *Through a Glass Darkly* (1961), and *David and Lisa* (1962). Among these, *The Snake Pit* provided viewers with the most hopeful outlook about the possibility of actually curing a person with a mental disorder; committed to a public mental institution by her husband, the suffering young woman is brought back to normalcy by therapy provided by a committed young doctor. I should add here that there

[13] Deutsch, p. 82.
[14] p. 96.
[15] p. 99.

were great numbers of other movies of the era – Westerns in which masses of people are slaughtered, domestic comedies full of anxiety-ridden people, satires like *Dr. Strangelove* (1964), a depiction of crazed academics like *Who's Afraid of Virginia Woolf* (1966) – in which characters (and social systems, too) are clearly unbalanced or insane, at least in the loose, nonclinical sense.

The phenomena of widespread juvenile delinquency and wide-spread mental illness were linked in 1950s discussions of "hipsters." As used at the time by those who approved of them – those who disapproved said they were bums, fakes, immature brats, hoodlums, and so on – a hipster was a person who was knowledgeable and alert as well as full of understanding.

The word had roots in American jazz of the 1940s and roots, therefore, in the black community, because jazz was originally an expressive musical form that arose from slavery and postslavery conditions. Jazz had become popularized earlier in the century and had been dominated in the 1930s and early 1940s, at least commercially, by largely or exclusively white "swing" bands. In the postwar years, a new jazz form, bop, or bebop, was on the cutting edge of jazz. The bop of musicians like Charlie Parker and Dizzy Gillespie was discordant, intense, and wildly improvisational. It was generally understood to be a rebellious rejection of conventional white jazz as well as conventional behavior. A July 3, 1948 *New Yorker* article on Dizzy Gillespie reported on the music as if it were a kind of political insurgency: "Boppers call themselves 'the left wing' and their opponents 'the right wing.' Friends of the older music call the beboppers 'dirty radicals' and wild-eyed revolutionaries.' Boppers are proud of the men that have gone without jobs and meals rather than play music that outraged their convictions, and speak indignantly of 'the underground.'"[16]

Hipsters, in brief, a largely young and white group, were associated with the rebelliousness of bop. The hipster was reported to speak a dialect that had first developed among black musicians. This sociolinguistic phenomenon was recognized in scholarly articles on

[16]   Richard O. Boyer, "Bop," *New Yorker*, 24 (July 3, 1948), pp. 28–32, 34–7.

the subject, including two in the journal *American Speech*, in December 1957 and October 1958.[17] Beyond language, according to newspaper and magazine and film accounts, the hipster was also likely to dress differently, to refuse to work, and to use drugs. A *Harper's Bazaar* article by Caroline Bird published in February 1957, remarked that "As the only extreme nonconformist of his generation, he exercises a powerful if underground appeal for conformists, through newspaper accounts of his delinquencies, his structureless jazz, and his emotive grunt words." Bird also commented that the hipster "may earn his living as a petty criminal, a hobo, a carnival roustabout or a free-lance moving man in Greenwich Village, but some hipsters have found a safe refuge in the upper income brackets as television comics or movie actors. (The late James Dean, for one, was a hipster hero)."[18]

Parts of Caroline Bird's article, including the descriptions I have quoted, were used as an epigraph by Norman Mailer in "The White Negro." That essay, first published in *Dissent* magazine in 1957, would become, at least among writers and intellectuals, the most influential account of hipsters, the "white negroes" of Mailer's title, and the huge social changes that they were said to represent. Mailer had established his literary reputation at the age of 25 with *The Naked and the Dead* (1948), considered by many to be the most distinguished of World War II combat novels. By the time he published "The White Negro," however, he was on his way to being known just as much for his own wild delinquencies as he was for his writing, and in the years and decades that followed his reputation as a kind of perennial *enfant terrible* continued to grow. In fact, as if the essay was not outrageous enough on its own, when he reprinted it in *Advertisements for Myself*, his 1959 book, he said that just before beginning it he had stopped using the drugs seconal and Benzedrine

[17] Robert S. Gold, "The Vernacular of the Jazz World," *American Speech*, 32, no. 4 (December 1957), pp. 271–82; Maurice A. Crane, "Vox Bop," *American Speech*, 33, no. 3 (October 1958), pp. 223–26.
[18] Caroline Bird, "Born 1930: The Unlost Generation," *Harper's Bazaar*, February 1957.

but had been "traveling [mentally] on marijuana."[19] This suggested
he was a great outlaw and rebel whose writing did not arise from
sober thought, a claim that seemed calculated to outrage reasonable
people who thought of writing as sober meditation done in calm
surroundings.

Mailer's starting point in "The White Negro" was his assertion
that the concentration camps of World War II and the atomic bombings of Japan that ended it presented a "mirror to the human condi-
tion" and that society was "murderous." As a result, he claimed,
dissent had become rare, for "A man knew that when he dissented,
he gave a note upon his life which could be called in any year of overt
crisis" and so, the post-war years had been "years of conformity and
depression": "A stench of fear has come out of every pore of American
life, and we suffer from a collective failure of nerve. The only courage,
with rare exceptions, that we have been witness to, has been the
isolated courage of isolated people." The hipster, Mailer said, knew
that, like others, he had few options. He could live awaiting "instant
death by atomic war, relatively quick death by the State as *l'univers
concentrationnaire*, or a slow death by conformity with every creative
and rebellious instinct stifled." Refusing death in these forms, the
hipster decided that "the only life-giving answer is to accept the
terms of death, to live with death as immediate danger, to divorce
oneself from society, to exist without roots, to set out on that
uncharted journey into the rebellious imperatives of the self." He
knew that he needed to "encourage the psychopath" in himself. He
knew that "one is a rebel or one conforms, one is a frontiersman in
the Wild West of American night life, or else a Square cell, trapped
in the totalitarian tissues of American society, doomed willy-nilly to
conform if one is to succeed."

Mailer made several claims in "The White Negro" that made even
his comment about the hipster as a "frontiersman in the Wild West
of American night life" seem restrained. The hipster, he said, had
come into being in places like New York's Greenwich Village when

[19]   Mailer, Introduction to "The White Negro," in *Advertisements for Myself*
(Putnam, New York, 1959), pp. 331–6.

"the bohemian and the juvenile delinquent came face-to-face with the Negro" and were married with a wedding ring made of marijuana. In one of several passages that must have struck many readers as outrageously racist as well as impossibly generalized from very thin evidence, he said that the Negro survived through "the art of the primitive" and

> subsisted for his Saturday night kicks, relinquishing the pleasures of the mind for the more obligatory pleasures of the body, and in his music he gave voice to the character and quality of his existence, to his rage and the infinite variations of joy, lust, languor, growl, cramp, pinch, scream and despair of his orgasm. For jazz is orgasm, it is the music of orgasm, good orgasm and bad. ...

Here, orgasm was obviously a metaphor. Later, Mailer described the negro-white negro-hipster-psychopath as a seeker after love but "Not love as the search for a mate, but love as the search for an orgasm more apocalyptic than the one which preceded it." Another passage spoke of the murder of a 50-year-old storekeeper by two strong 18-year-old psychopathic hoodlums and concluded that it took courage "of a sort" to commit the murder because "one murders not only a weak fifty-year-old man but an institution as well, one violates private property, one enters into a new relation with the police and introduces a dangerous element into one's life."[20]

"Psychopath" was sometimes used broadly, to mean a mentally unstable person. But in the psychiatric literature of the period, with which Mailer was familiar, a "psychopath" had criminal propensities and an "antisocial" mentality. Psychopaths were likely to have come from broken homes and never to have been exposed to consistent training because of the absence of stable parental figures, to have suffered childhood deprivations, to have presented discipline problems to teachers and other authorities, and to have spent some time in an institution. As an adult, the psychopath was impulsive and in

[20] Mailer, "The White Negro," in *Advertisements for Myself* (Putnam, New York, 1959), pp. 338–58.

search of immediate gratification, unable to commit to steady employment, unable to conform to social rules, unable to have prolonged or deep personal attachments, and was often sexually promiscuous.

The Literature

Postwar American literature is populated by juvenile offenders, wildly rebellious young men, young men victimized by American society, hipsters traveling in constellations disconnected from mainstream society, young and old people suffering from some sort of mental illness. A person reading through the classic texts of the era might justly ask questions like "Where were the good boys and men?", or "Who was sane or balanced in these imagined worlds?" A reader might also wonder about the visions of America contained in the literature and ask questions like "Was the country really so dumb and unenlightened, was it really so repressive?".

Juvenile offenders or victims were central figures in such short stories as Terry Southern's "Red-Dirt Marijuana" and "A South Summer Idyll," Michael Rumaker's "The Truck," John Updike's "The Hillies," Joyce Carol Oates's "Boys at a Picnic," and Grace Paley's "The Little Girl." Updike's "The Hillies," written in 1969, depicts alienated young people living on a hillside in a small town north of Boston and the reactions to them by various townspeople in letters to the editor of a local newspaper. Those reactions represent perfectly the range of adult responses to juvenile delinquency, explaining it as just rebellions, an effort to save the world from self-destruction, as an inexplicable responses to good upbringings, and so forth. A letter signed by 16 of the hillies repeats the sort of explanation stated frequently in movies, other fiction, and popular sociology: "they just want to sit and 'dig." Dig? 'Life as it just is,' the letter … concludes, 'truly grooves.'" The Paley story is an especially penetrating account of the brutal rape and murder of a teenage runaway. Truman Capote's *In Cold Blood* (1966) placed great emphasis on the family backgrounds of its two young killers of a Kansas family of four.

The most graphic account of the brutality of teenagers and young men (and of older men and women, too) is in the linked stories of Hubert Selby, Jr's *Last Exit to Brooklyn* (1964). Set during and just after World War II, written entirely in vulgar slang, the stories offer none of the usual explanations or rationalizations (except the desire for "kicks" and money) for any of the brutal behavior depicted. The story "Another Day, Another Dollar" depicts the brutalities inflicted on soldiers outside a Brooklyn army base by utterly amoral street-corner thugs. Another story, "Tralala," depicts a teenage prostitute's anger and brutality that ends only when she is brutally gang raped in a horrifyingly graphic scene. I once tried teaching "Tralala" to a group of undergraduate students, many of whom found it over-whelming and some of whom found it simply too disturbing to finish reading. I do not think it is likely that the story will appear anytime soon in a college or high school anthology.

Ann Petry's story "The Witness," written in the late 1960s but not published until 1971, focused on delinquent boys whose parents were "the backbone of the great middle class" in an upstate New York small town. The leader of the group is said to have an IQ in the "genius bracket" and the group demonstrates considerable creative nastiness in dealing with the adults who are trying to civilize them. The most anthologized of delinquency stories, "The Witness" provides a full description of the uniform postures, dress, hairdos, clothing, and partially "black" language inflections of the boys, all of which threatens adults. The "witness" of the story is Charles Woodruff, a retired college professor from Virginia who has been hired to teach English at the town high school. Woodruff is the only black in the town, but he appears to have been widely accepted with "genuine friendliness," his students liked him and told him so, and the minister who is trying to reach the delinquent boys has asked for his assistance.

The story turns on the apparent gang rape of a girl witnessed by Woodruff. I say "apparent" because just prior to it the girl is described as waiting in a snowstorm for the boys to finish their class with the minister and Woodruff, and it is indicated that she has had sex with the boys on other occasions. Also she is dressed exactly like them and combs her hair like them, indicating her membership in the group, and the day after the apparent gang rape she is riding in the front seat of the boys' car. On the other hand, a gang rape may actually have happened, the girl may have been an actual victim (or serial victim) whose "consent" and group membership was manipulated by the clever delinquents in an adolescent version of the so-called Stockholm Syndrome. While the term Stockholm Syndrome was not coined or defined until 1973, several years after the story was written, perhaps Petry had some intuition about such behaviors.

"The Witness" also turns on Woodruff's capacity as an observer and accurate reporter of events and his capacity as a judge of character. From everything we are told about him, he is a poor witness, a weak observer. He certainly has no objectivity, for despite the friendly acceptance he has received from the town, he imagines racist police responses to him, imagines he is the "nigger in the woodpile," and thinks of his "hard-working, courteous" students as "pathetic." At one point he thinks of the delinquents as the "white man's problem." At another, he shows his absolute prejudice against them when he says that all of them were white but "there was about them an aura of something so evil, so dark, so suggestive of the far reaches of the night, of the black horror of nightmares, that he shivered deep inside himself whenever he saw them." The reversals involved in that passage, in which a black man describes white boys in the racist terms traditionally used by whites to describe blacks, suggests a great deal about the prejudiced workings of Woodruff's mind, as do a number of other similar comments (including his comments on the distinct unclean smells of white teenagers), as do the indications that he is unable to stay focused on the present because he is drawn to memories of his past life. But Petry also provides a simpler reason for distrusting Woodruff. As the central event begins to unfold, the delinquents break his glasses. Without them he was "half-blind" and "uncertain of the shape of objects" and is, therefore, totally unreliable as a witness.

"The Witness" is a fine story about privileged white delinquents and about how one man, who happens to be black, perceives or misperceives them. It is also a story which argues that after a lifetime of living in a racist society a black person cannot simply adapt to being accepted by a white community, even (or perhaps especially) a white community which has hired him as its one black teacher. Nor can a black person perceive white children, good ones or delinquents, fairly and without prejudice, because whether or not a gang rape actually happens, as Woodruff understands, he will be accused of breaking the taboo of touching a white woman and the sullenly crazed delinquents who will be witnesses against him will be believed. This may sound paranoid to some readers, but paranoia can be an appropriate response to a world full of insane assailants.

Jack Kerouac's *On the Road* was the postwar period's most discussed and influential account of rampaging, troubled, alienated, seeking, and sometimes sweetly romantic young people. Published in 1957, a few months after Mailer's "The White Negro" appeared, *On the Road* focused on the exploits of two young men, Dean Moriarty and Sal Paradise, in the years between 1947 and 1950. The story is narrated by Sal, who is about 25 in 1947. Sal was raised by his aunt – he never mentions his parents – in the mill city of Paterson, NJ. He was in the service during the war, attends Columbia University, off and on, under the GI Bill, has read considerably, is an aspiring writer, and near the end of the novel mentions that he has sold a book.

Sal has a conventional outlook. Early in the book, he comments on his great desire to find the right girl and to settle down. He also comments on casual sex, saying "Boys and girls in America have such a sad time together; sophistication demands that they submit to sex immediately without proper preliminary talk," by which he means "Not courting talk – real straight talk about souls, for life is holy and every moment is precious." Sometimes he is confused and lost. He confesses that he fears attacks by "queers," carrying a gun into San Francisco bars even though he "knew queers all over the country." Sal also often seems fragile. Just before he meets Terry, the first of his girlfriends in the novel, he describes himself as "so lonely, so sad, so tired, so quivering, so broken, so beat," and on many other occasions he describes himself as "sad." But we are told little about what may have caused his problems. Do they derive from his upbringing?

The closest we are brought to possible family problems is when he says that "Everything I had ever secretly held against my brother was coming out: how ugly I was and what filth I was discovering in the depths of my own impure psychologies" but that statement is vague. Do his problems derive from his wartime service? The only detail we have about his wartime service is one memory of drinking 60 glasses of beer in a Boston bar, drunkenly passing out with his body wrapped around the men's toilet, and waking up with the realization that "at least" a hundred seaman and civilians had gone to the toilet *on* him, leaving him "unrecognizably caked."

Dean Moriarty is 19 or 20 in 1947. His teenage years conform to standard popular press and movie accounts of the juvenile delinquent. His mother died when he was very young and he was raised by his hard-drinking father, mostly in Denver and in California, until he was 11, when he was abandoned or lost by the father. He then lived on his own, shoplifted a good deal, stole cars, and spent about five years in reformatories and jail.

In *On the Road*, Dean is all passion and impulsive energy. He loves driving fast. He loves drinking and listening to jazz. He loves parties and "kicks." He is driven by sex, by "that lil ole gal with that lil sumpin down there tween her legs, boy." All of this passion and energy is present-oriented; he has no thoughts about the consequences of his actions, and so he leaves friends in the lurch and has no regard for his children or, once he has found another woman, for his current woman. Dean is no mystery to other characters. His women understand his irresponsibility quite well, though they cannot resist him. The character Roland Major says he is a "moron and fool." The character Bull Lee, who is based on the writer William J. Burroughs, provides a clinical-sounding assessment: "He seems to me to be headed for his ideal fate, which is compulsive psychosis dashed with a jigger of psychopathic irresponsibility and violence."

Sal is sometimes hurt by Dean although he understands his irresponsibility. But Sal also maintains that Dean is special, that he is a mad genius, and at various points in the novel, in the midst of frenetic action, he tries to analyze the stages of Dean's comet-like passage through the world. Near the beginning, he says that Dean has "the tremendous energy of a new kind of American saint." At the beginning of the second part, after noticing that Dean had become increasingly frenetic and agitated in his physical movements, he says that "these were the first days of his mysticism." Further on, Sal describes him in his "final development" as "BEAT – the root, the soul of Beatific" and remarks that "Bitterness, recriminations, advice, morality, sadness – everything was behind him, and ahead of him was the ragged and ecstatic joy of pure being." During this "mystic stage," Sal says that Dean makes "Tao decisions" and Dean says of himself that "I've decided to leave everything out of my hands. *You've* seen me try to break my ass to make it and know that it doesn't matter and we know time – how to slow it up and walk and dig and just old-fashioned spade [i.e., black] kicks, what other kicks are there? *We* know." Dean's "ecstatic joy of pure being" also yields language like "God! Yes!" and "he knows time" and "that alto [saxophonist] had IT – he held it once he found it; I've never seen a guy who could hold it that long."

Sal is very impressed with Dean's language and, while retaining a command of standard English, sometimes adopts Dean's expressive ecstasy. Smoking marijuana in Mexico, for instance, he realizes that "In myriad pricklings of heavenly radiation I had to struggle to see Dean's figure, and he looked like God." On another occasion, he describes how he has fused with Dean and how the two now "swayed to the rhythm and the IT of our final excited joy in talking and living to the blank tranced end of all innumerable riotous angelic particulars that had been lurking in our souls all our lives." That kind of writing may have been influenced by earlier attempts by writers to express the "nonrational" and the mystic – for example, surrealist writing, various Modernist texts, Whitman, William Blake, Arthur Rimbaud, Hart Crane, Allen Ginsberg – but the more immediate inspiration within *On the Road* is bop. Sal refers to bop as "the sound of the night" which represents his generation, and there are long passages in later parts of the novel, such as in chapters 4 and 10 of Part 3, some describing inspirational bop musicians and others trying to accurately describe the sounds and syncopations of bop. The core idea seems to be that a person can set the rules of discourse aside to find new energies in language in the same way that bop musicians can invent new sounds. Involved with this idea is the proposition that the hipster in the world of bop, like the musicians themselves, can also put aside the rules governing socially acceptable behavior, thereby outraging conventional people, and create a radically new subculture.

On the Road does not contain very much explicit commentary on what ails America. "Normal" lives and places are barely mentioned and only a few brief passages provide a picture of the culture. The character Bull Lee, who is said to be a teacher of young men like Sal, says that the American economy is fraudulent because the know-how exists to make things last forever but "They prefer making cheap goods so everybody'll have to go on working and punching timeclocks and organizing themselves in sullen unions and floundering around while the big grab goes on in Washington." Sal makes a few remarks about the culture in general. Americans, he says, spend their lives doing "what they think they're supposed to do" and "everybody in America is a natural-born thief" and "arty types" are "all over America, sucking its blood." Regarding social order, he says, unfair and mean police "are involved in psychological warfare against those Americans who don't frighten them with imposing papers and threats." There are also a few comments regarding the national posture at the beginning of the Cold War. One occurs when, passing through Washington, DC on Inauguration Day, 1948, Sal and Dean see "all kinds of war material that looked murderous in the snowy grass; the last thing was a regular small ordinary lifeboat that looked pitiful and foolish," and Dean says that President Truman must know that, despite all the weaponry, he will need a lifeboat when the end of civilization comes. Another comes near the novel's end, when Sal says, probably in a reference to the Soviet Union having created its own nuclear bomb in August 1949, that the US would soon be as poor as Mexico, because "a bomb had come that could crack all our bridges and roads and reduce them to jumbles."

Allen Ginsberg's first book, *Howl and Other Poems* (1956), dedicated to Kerouac, Burroughs, and Neal Cassady (the real-life Dean

Moriarty), and introduced by William Carlos Williams, contains a brilliant vision of America similar to Sal's but far more specific about the country's repressiveness, the banal, dead conformity of its people, its destruction of its "best minds" and its creation of crazed people, its madhouse character and its actual madhouses, its institutions, full of tortured people being given electroshock therapy.

Whatever America is or is not, whether Dean is a juvenile delinquent despite his chronological age, a psychopath or a saint, an irresponsible destroyer or a bringer of truth and wisdom, Sal Paradise learns from his experience that he does not want to be a white man. This is at least marginally clear when, after falling into the life of a farm laborer while he was with Terry, he refers to his fellow laborers and their families as "we Mexicans" and says that local "Okies" "thought I was Mexican, of course; and in a way I am." It is clear in all of his comments on bop music and culture. It is abundantly clear at the beginning of Part 3, when he talks about "wishing I were a Negro" and a bit later about wishing to be "a Denver Mexican, or even a poor overworked Jap, anything but what I was so drearily, a 'white man' disillusioned" and, at the end of the passage, about wishing to "exchange worlds with the happy, true-hearted, ecstatic Negroes of America." I think I understand what Sal meant. I think I also understand that the passage is culturally very significant because it is one of the first times, if not the very first time, that a post-World War II American writer expressed what so many white Americans of later years also expressed, an identification with black as opposed to white culture. Nonetheless, I think I have groaned out loud every time I have ever read that passage to myself, and I know that I have blushed when I had to deal with it in classrooms, mostly because of Sal's complete swallowing of the racist American myth of the happy Negro.

There are no black writers who share Kerouac's sense of life in the black community. Rather, to generalize, most black writers understand the profound distorting effects of insane white people and white racism on the psychological and social well-being of black (and white) people. This was the subject of Ralph Ellison's "Harlem is Nowhere," a short essay about the Larfargue Psychiatric Clinic of

Harlem written in 1948 while he was working on *Invisible Man*.[21]
Ellison of course understood the positive aspects of Harlem life and
the strength of black culture. But much of his essay described the
negative aspects of Harlem, including its "crimes, its casual violence,
its crumbling buildings with littered areaways, ill-smelling halls, and
vermin-invaded rooms" and the "surreal fantasies" acted out on its
streets. Harlem's energy was taken up with efforts to "overcome the
frustrations of social discrimination." Great numbers of its people
were confused, bewildered, frustrated, and enraged. The Psychiatric
Clinic, according to Ellison, staffed by psychiatrists who volunteered
their services, was an institution that recognized that "the personality
damage that brought it into being represents not the disintegration
of a people's fiber, but the failure of a way of life." Individual madness
manifested on the streets of Harlem, including the multiple identities
of the proto-hipster Rinehart, group madness in the form of a race
riot, as well as the lunatic ideological certitudes of the Communist
Party, are central to *Invisible Man*. The parts of the book that take
place in the South are also filled with mentally ill people.

The destruction of black humanity by racism can be seen in much
black writing of the postwar period. Ann Petry's *The Street* (1946)
was perhaps the most derailed of novels about black Harlem. James
Baldwin's "Sonny's Blues," a 1957 story set in Harlem, is filled with
enraged youngsters whose "heads bumped abruptly against the low
ceilings of their actual possibilities" and pictures of "vivid, killing
streets." The father of the family had watched the gratuitous murder
of his brother on a road in the South and, according to the mother,
he "never did really get right again. Till the day he died he weren't
sure but that every white man he saw was the man that killed his
brother." The older son, the narrator, becomes a teacher, a profession that "raises" him but at the same time distorts his ability to
understand his community. The younger son, Sonny, drops out of
high school, becomes a heroin user, and then later discovers himself
in jazz.

[21]   Ralph Ellison, "Harlem is Nowhere," in *The Collected Essays of Ralph Ellison*
(Modern Library, New York, 1995), pp. 320–7.

In such iconic poems as "The Sundays of Satin-Legs Smith," "The Mother," "We Real Cool," and "The Last Quatrain of the Ballad of Emmett Till," Gwendolyn Brooks wrote incisively about the crippling psychological effects of racism, as did poets like Sonia Sanchez and Etheridge Knight. The exploitation of black male sexuality by murderous white women and the distorting appropriation of elements of black culture by a crazed, murderous white society was brilliantly explored by Amiri Baraka in his one-act play, *Dutchman* (1964). The soliloquy at the end of that play, a penetrating account of the insane racist white American society and the "madness" of black people, included a prediction that, after being educated to Western rationalism, blacks would behave just like whites: "They'll murder you, and have very rational explanations. Very much like your own. They'll cut your throats, and drag you out to the edge of your cities so the flesh can fall away from your bones, in sanitary isolation."

In addition to the literature I have already mentioned or discussed in some detail, there are many other postwar works, some of which have become classics, that involve delinquency or madness or both. J. D. Salinger's *The Catcher in the Rye* (1951) became the most popular depiction of a troubled adolescent ever published. Vladimir Nabokov's *Lolita* (1955) was a complex story of a European pedophile's obsessive involvement with a young girl who is, as pictured by him, both his victim and his seductress; *Lolita* also includes an on-the-road narrative, a travel account of life across America among the allegedly normal folk. Philip Roth's *Portnoy's Complaint* (1969) is a narration by an inflamed, obsessed, and mother-maddened boy-man who objectifies all women as sexual objects, who was sexually adventurous (and creative) even as a child, and who, ironically, now works as the Assistant Commissioner for New York's Commission on Human Opportunity. Some of the greatest plays of the era – for example, Miller's *Death of a Salesman*, Tennessee Williams's *Suddenly, Last Summer* and *The Glass Menagerie* and many others, Edward Albee's *Who's Afraid of Virginia Woolf* – are dramas of people who were born mad or driven mad. Charles Bukowski's many books of poems, and fictions such as *Post Office* (1971), featured speakers who were in a state of perpetual boyish rebelliousness and terminal outrageousness.

Ken Kesey's *One Flew Over the Cuckoo's Nest* (1962) was one of the most popular postwar fictions to make the argument that normalcy was often madness and that madness could be inspired. Set in a psychiatric ward of a veterans administration hospital, the novel pits the wild, profane, imaginative, and humane Randle Patrick McMurphy, the initials of whose name stand for the measure of energy "revolutions per minute," against the cruel representative of the repressive state, Big Nurse Ratched, whose surname suggests a ratchet wrench, a tool to curtail movement. Many of the ward residents are relatively sane in comparison to their keepers and some of the therapies used by the keepers are cruelties. Electroshock therapy is used as a weapon by the Big Nurse so that McMurphy will be prompted to realize his mistakes and, when that does not work, McMurphy is lobotomized to serve as a symbol to other recalcitrant patients of the ultimate cost of rebellion. The normal workaday world outside the hospital is rarely glimpsed – the hospital *is* the universe – but when it is, it is represented as robotized: on his one trip out of the ward, the narrator sees "a *train* stopping at a station and laying a string of full-grown men in mirrored suits and machined hats, laying them like a hatch of identical insects, half-life things coming pht-pht-pht out of the last car, then hooting its electric whistle and moving on down the spoiled land to deposit another hatch." These insects are suburban commuters, of course.

Kesey had worked as an attendant in a veterans administration hospital while a graduate student in the late 1950s. Just before he took that job, he had been a paid volunteer in a government-funded project testing the effects of hallucinogenic drugs. Later, he became one of the leaders of the American drug culture that viewed LSD and other hallucinogens as the means through which the individual mind would be altered, made whole and pure, and become capable of viewing the world in all its alleged psychedelic glory. Kesey's years as the leader of the so-called Merry Pranksters, a group of acidhead pioneers which for a time included the beat hero Neal Cassady (i.e.,

Dean Moriarty), was chronicled by Tom Wolfe in *The Electric Kool-Aid Acid Test* (1968).

In the work of Sylvia Plath, who knew more at a personal level about mental illness in general and depression in particular than any of her contemporaries I have discussed, there was no rebellious fun, there were no inspired madmen, and no drug-induced epiphanies. Plath struggled with depression and went through a severe depressive episode in 1953. Later, she worked in the records office for mental patients in Massachusetts General Hospital, a job that led to her 1957 story "Johnny Panic and the Bible of Dreams." Her iconic novel *The Bell Jar*, based on her 1953 experience, which was published under a pseudonym in England in 1963, was as sharp and sober an account of mental illness as any book published by a postwar American writer. Its main character, Esther Greenwood, a gifted college student, was shown going through the early stages of depression, then falling into a fearsome deep depression for which she was hospitalized and at first received inadequate treatment, then being brought back out of the depression by a smart psychiatrist who knew how to properly administer electrotherapy. In that regard, much like the film *The Snake Pit*, *The Bell Jar* was an inspirational story about good psychiatry and its promise for people suffering from depression and also because it showed a young woman awakening from her ordeal intent on forging a free and equal womanhood based on her own definitions of sexuality and the meaning of marriage and family in her life.

The causes of Esther's depression are unclear. The novel includes a number of images and motifs that suggest that there were definable causes: for example, an overbearing mother, a number of inadequate and insensitive men, personality-crushing sexual repressions and double standards, too great a devotion to study, the June 1953 executions of the Rosenbergs that occurs on the first page of the novel and that are remembered later. The novel, though, also argues that depression is not the cumulative effect of clear causes outside the mind but, rather, strikes its sufferers without warning and for no "reason" whatsoever and is therefore another treacherous hazard in a bad and mad world.

A Brief Comment on 1960s Youth Radicalism and Anti-Vietnam War Writing

Through the 1950s, it was commonplace to say that US society was sick. To many Americans, events and trends in the 1960s indicated that the sickness was accelerating and deepening. President John F. Kennedy, Malcolm X, Martin Luther King, Jr., and Senator Robert Kennedy were all assassinated between 1963 and 1968. Hundreds of riots and other civil disturbances occurred in a number of cities (I will discuss some of them in the next chapter). Crime rates increased. Drug use was rampant. The so-called "generation gap," the cultural and other differences between young and old, loomed ever larger.

There was a huge amount of contemporary journalistic and social science analysis of what was happening in the country. There was also an enormous amount of commentary of various sorts, all of it rebellious or revolutionary, published in "underground" newspapers and magazines. In later decades, the impact of the 1960s on American society would continue to be discussed in a never-ending torrent of memoirs and histories, political commentaries, and films. In many accounts, the "Sixties" became a code word that meant either pure liberation or grotesque distortion.

The "New Left" of the 1960s began with the founding of Students for a Democratic Society (SDS) in 1962 by a group of college and graduate students. The SDS "Port Huron Statement," its manifesto and program for action, began by describing the two most "troubling" issues of the time, the "permeating and victimizing fact of human degradation, symbolized by the Southern struggle against racial bigotry" and the "enclosing fact of the Cold War, symbolized by the presence of the Bomb." It described the empty lives of Americans, their anxieties, hopelessness, fear of change, and "indifference to human affairs." Most importantly, it discussed the alternative

values it intended to inculcate through its work. The early ide-
alism of SDS was captured in a paragraph that introduced the
specific reforms it sought:

> We would replace power rooted in possession, privilege, or
> circumstance by power and uniqueness rooted in love,
> reflectiveness, reason, and creativity. As a *social system* we
> seek the establishment of a democracy of individual partici-
> pation, governed by two central aims: that the individual
> share in those social decisions determining the quality and
> direction of his life; that society be organized to encourage
> independence in men and provide the media for their
> common participation.[22]

Over the decade after its founding, because of events, the
resistance of the political establishment, and the resistance of
those it proposed to save from their empty lives, SDS would
become considerably more hard-bitten and cynical. But the
"Port Huron Statement" suggests the hopeful note on which it
began.

In the "Port Huron Statement" and later writing, SDS also
argued that colleges and universities were centers of political
and social power which, like other centers of power, needed to
be reformed if not revolutionized. It thus joined, and sometimes led, a broad movement which maintained that adminis-
trators and faculties unjustly controlled the lives of their
students, treated them as children, forced them to take irrelevant courses, and attempted to regulate their off-campus
behavior. The perception of "totalitarian" practices by colleges
and universities led to sharp, well-publicized protests such as
the 1964 "Free Speech Movement" at the University of
California at Berkeley. Protests were soon mounted on some

[22] The text of the "Port Huron Statement" can be found at http://history.hanover.
edu/courses/excerpts/111hur.html

campuses around other issues, though by 1966, directly and indirectly, the Vietnam War was a major issue in a great number of campus protests. The immediate local targets often included science professors who did research for the Department of Defense and other government entities and were thus involved in work vital to the waging of the war; the Army's Reserve Officers Training Corp (ROTC), which had large student enrollments on campuses through which the Army got many of its officers; and manufacturers of war materiel like Dow Chemical, which recruited employees on campuses.

The tendency of urban universities to gobble up the land of their poor and weak neighbors – many urban institutions were located in or near black neighborhoods – for new building projects was the direct cause for a number of significant protests in the later 1960s, including the widely reported one at Columbia University in New York. The strike at San Francisco State University during the 1968–69 academic year, which involved students, faculty, labor unions, and communities far beyond the campus, was the most complex and multidimensional of the campus protests. A central issue in the strike was the situations of blacks on campus and the future of black and ethnic studies. The original written demands of the Black Student Union, the original "convener" of the strike, included items such as the centralization of all black studies courses in a black studies department, the promotion of the chair of that department to full professor, the allocation of 20 new teaching positions to the department, and the admission of all black students who applied to Berkeley for the Fall of 1969.

In making such demands, opponents said, students were trying to substitute their judgment for that of professionals. Student leaders, who often sounded well-steeped in the contemporary literature which argued that the world young people were going to inherit was sick, responded that the professionals were poor judges and, worse, members of the corrupt

"Establishment" that oppressed students as much as it oppressed black people and other minorities. That response was fleshed out by Jerry Farber, an instructor of English at one of the California state colleges, in his 1967 essay "The Student as Nigger," which circulated around the country in several hundred alternative press reprintings and in other forms such as mimeographing. Farber was straightforward about the oppression of students, listing several clear signs that students existed as powerless slaves. But he was not sanguine about revolutionary possibilities:

> As do black slaves, students vary in their awareness of what's going on. Some recognize their own put-on for what it is and even let their rebellion break through to the surface now and then. Others – including most of the "good students" – have been more deeply brain washed. They swallow the bullshit with greedy mouths. They honest-to-God believe in grades, in busy work, in General Education requirements. They're like those old grey-headed house niggers you can still find in the South who don't see what all the fuss is about because Mr. Charlie "treats us real good."

Moreover, Farber wrote, their teachers, who should be their allies in rebellion, were for the most part silent about the issues of the day, including the Vietnam War. This led him to declare that he did not know why teachers were so "chickenshit" but "It could be that academic training itself forces a split between thought and action. It might also be that the tenured security of a teaching job attracts timid persons and, furthermore, that teaching, like police work, pulls in persons who are unsure of themselves and need weapons and the other external trappings of authority."[23]

[23] Farber, "The Student as Nigger," can be found at http://ry4an.org/readings/short/student/

Farber's frustrated comments on brainwashed students and silent teachers, I think, reflect the fact that campus protests (and youth radicalism generally) in the 1960s was a minority affair. That is, as I understand the history, places like Columbia, Berkeley, San Francisco State, and Wisconsin were very unusual. The great majority of faculty did not proselytize their students to rebel, and the great majority of students did not protest anything. All dissident movements exaggerate their numbers and power, of course, just as their opponents exaggerate the threats posed by them to decency, order, and well-being. This rule of thumb especially applies when the mass public has become used, year after year and decade after decade, to hearing tales of juvenile delinquency and youthful excesses.

White radical youth of the era often looked to young radical blacks for intellectual leadership. The Student Non-Violent Coordinating Committee (SNCC), which orchestrated the Freedom Rides beginning in the spring of 1961, was the early inspiration for the white student movement that crested in the 1964 "Mississippi Summer" in which more than 1,000 northern college students went to that state to do community organizing and voter registration. The admiration of radicalized white students for SNCC abated somewhat, but not entirely, when SNCC decided to rid itself of white influence, arguing that whites needed to go into their own racist communities to change them instead of working in black communities. Radical separatism was justified in a 1966 SNCC essay titled "The Basis of Black Power," which said that "If we are to proceed toward true liberation, we must cut ourselves off from white people. We must form our own institutions, credit unions, co-ops, political parties, write our own histories."[24] H. Rap Brown, one of the leaders of the Black Power movement, writing in his *Die,*

[24] "The Basis of Black Power" can be found at http://www2.iath.virginia.edu/sixties/HTML_docs/Resources/Primary/Manifestos/SNCC_black_power.html

Nigger, Die! (1970), struck one of his most bellicose notes when he wrote:

> Our job is not to convert whites. If whites are dedicated to revolution then they can be used in the struggle. However, if they impede the struggle and are proven to be a problem then it is up to us to deal with them as with all problems. Our job now is to project what should be our common goal – the destruction of a system that makes slavery possible.[25]

Similar separatist and militant beliefs infused the rhetoric of the Black Panthers. Picturing black communities as colonies subjugated and exploited by white people, it proposed to lead blacks in an anticolonial uprising toward self-determination. Words like "revolution" and "destruction," and talk about carrying arms (for self-defense against racist police, it was usually said) became increasingly common in the rhetoric of black radicals. Some white radicals of the later 1960s, such as the Weather Underground, a group which split from the SDS over the issue of revolutionary tactics, used similar rhetoric and, from time to time, from 1969 to the mid-1970s, sought to bring about change through violent methods such as armed robberies to finance the revolution, bombings, attacks on police and judges, and so forth. Predictably, the government, police forces and the media – just as had been done in response to nineteenth-century and early twentieth-century anarchists, to the IWW in the World War I years, and to the CPUSA – used the new propensity to violence among some radicals as evidence of the violence and un-Americanness of *all* radicals.

---

[25] From H. Rap Brown, *Die, Nigger, Die* (Allison and Busby, London, 1970); reprinted in Loren Baritz (ed.) *The American Left: Radical Political Thought in the Twentieth Century* (Basic Books, New York and London, 1971), pp. 370–3. The quote is from p. 371.

Hippies sometimes sounded even more revolutionary than Black Panthers, Black Power advocates, and SDS radicals. But while arguably politically oriented because they were so anti-Establishment, hippies were scarcely interested in policy issues and community organizing. Earlier, I mentioned Tom Wolfe's 1968 portrait of Ken Kesey and the "Merry Pranksters" in his *The Electric Kool-Aid Acid Test*. Similar accounts appeared in the mainstream press, whose readers had a great appetite for reading about hippies; for a few years, many alternative newspapers were dominated by hippie concerns and effusive hippie poetry and art. Warren Hinckle's essay "A Social History of the Hippies," which appeared first in the magazine *Ramparts* in 1967, offered a penetrating description of the "psychedelic bohemia" hippies had established in San Francisco:

> There, in a daily street-fair atmosphere, upwards of fifteen thousand unbounded girls and boys interact in a tribal, love-free, free-swinging, acid-based type of society where, if you are a hippie and you have a dime, you can put it in a parking meter and lie down in the street for an hour's suntan (thirty minutes for a nickel) and most drivers will be careful not to run you over.

Hinckle, however, deplored hippie "quietism" – its turned-on, tuned-in, disengaged lifestyle – and warned in the last paragraph of his essay that if hippie "quietism" spread further "the future of activist, serious politics is bound to be affected."[26]

Like the outside world against which it so mightily protested, the 1960s radical movements were male-dominated, hierarchical, and patriarchic. Ken Kesey's sexual exploitation of some of his female followers was a subtheme in Wolfe's account. Black Panther Party leader Eldridge Cleaver in his *Soul on Ice* (1968)

[26] Warren Hinckle, "A Social History of the Hippies," *Ramparts* 6 (March, 1970), pp. 5–26.

wrote of his past belief that rape was an "insurrectionary act" (his repudiation of this thinking struck some readers as insincere or was not even noticed). But women in the movement did not need such famous instances to begin to protest against the degradations of women by their male colleagues, whose own behavior, they said, had little connection to their talk of love, equality, and freedom. In a 1968 essay, "The Look is You," SDS women Naomi Jaffe and Bernadine Dohrn remarked that "we are unfree within the movement and in personal relationships, as in the society at large" while calling for a broad new social movement for women's liberation.[27] In other of the founding documents of what would later become radical feminism, there was a similar understanding. In their 1969 essay "Bread and Roses," Kathy McAfee and Myrna Wood recognized that even in advanced socialist countries such as Cuba, Vietnam, and China the full liberation of women had been instigated by militant women and that "liberation is not handed down from above."[28] In her 1970 "Goodbye to All That," Robin Morgan brilliantly pilloried the male chauvinist attitudes of radical men and said that "It is the job of revolutionary feminists to build an ever stronger independent Women's Liberation Movement." Morgan announced near the end of her essay: "Goodbye, goodbye forever, counterfeit left, counterfeit, male-dominated cracked-glass mirror reflection of the Amerikan Nightmare."[29] The German spelling of "Amerika," here as elsewhere in radical writing of the period, was code for saying the US was now a Nazi state and implied that men of the movement were Nazis too.

---

[27] From Naomi Jaffe and Bernadine Dohrn, "The Look is You: Toward a Strategy for Radical Women," *New Left Notes* (March 18, 1968); reprinted in Baritz (ed.) *The American Left*, pp. 473–77. The quote is from p. 473.

[28] The text of the essay can be found at http://scriptorium.lib.duke.edu/wlm/mcafee/

[29] Robin Morgan, "Goodbye to All That," *Rat* (January, 1970); in Baritz (ed.) *The American Left*, pp. 501–7. The quote is from p. 507.

During the Eisenhower and Kennedy Administrations, American involvement in Vietnam had been relatively minor. Between 1966 and 1968, under President Johnson, the war escalated dramatically, accompanied by a series of well-documented government policy failures, horrifying images of death and destruction carried into American homes by television news, and large antiwar demonstrations. Those demonstrations and other antiwar efforts bound together the various strands of 1960s radicalism – whatever their differences on matters of "quietism" and engagement, degrees of militance, the wisdom of separatism, the chauvinism of radical men, and so forth, all agreed that Vietnam was an evil, inhumane war. Many agreed that Vietnam also demonstrated the moral bankruptcy of the Establishment, the failure of American foreign policy, the inevitable result of American paranoia about Communism, and the violent tendencies buried deep in the American psyche.

Founded in 1966 by Robert Bly and David Ray, a group called American Writers Against the Vietnam War organized antiwar poetry readings on college campuses and at other places. Often involving antiwar testimonials by the writers as well as organizing activities by members of the audience, the readings brought together prominent poets such as Bly himself, Denise Levertov, Allen Ginsberg, Robert Duncan, Robert Creeley, Galway Kinnell, and James Wright. The basic idea behind them was to get writers and other intellectuals involved in the antiwar movement, which meant getting them to reengage as intellectual leaders after many years of political disengagement. In a 1967 collection titled *A Poetry Reading Against the Vietnam War*, Bly wrote about the crucial role of intellectuals: "It becomes more and more clear that the United States is not stable; if there were no intellectual community, the United States would be capable of anything. The American public, the non-intellectual community, will swallow whatever Washington rolls up to its mouth, The old description the Czechs used to give around 1950 of their puppet legislatures begins to fit the

American public: one half incapable of anything, and the other half capable of anything." Bly's statement, which was echoed by many other antiwar writers, obviously expressed a considerable amount of doubt about the basic goodness and decency of "everyday" or "ordinary" people and it expressed considerable faith in intellectuals. That was a sharp reversal of the positions of earlier engaged writers who argued that the people were to be trusted, while the intellectuals were to be entirely distrusted because they were removed from the actualities of life.

A Poetry Reading Against the Vietnam War included poems by long-dead poets, recent poems by contemporaries, quotations from politicians, statements about their love of peace by tyrants such as Adolf Hitler, a statement by Freud about how societies decline when men and women make no objections to tyranny, a number of attacks on President Johnson, a statement by journalist I. F. Stone saying that "The No. 1 problem of humanity is to contain the United States," a quotation from a US pilot, originally published in the July 6, 1965 *New York Times*, which said, "I don't like to hit a village. You know you are hitting women and children, too. But you've got to decide your work is noble and that the work has to be done," and several comments on the horrifying civilian casualties in Vietnam, many of them the result of incendiary bombings. This was a fairly representative cross-section of what was said during the campus poetry readings. It was also a fairly accurate sampling of the chief points made by the 1960s antiwar movement in general.

The bombings in Vietnam and its neighboring countries of Laos and Cambodia were often used by writers and other antiwar protesters as proof that the American conduct of the war was criminal and genocidal. Reports of massive air raids were constant in the press. By 1972, there were widely accepted statistics regarding the extent of the bombings. According to a respected Cornell University study titled *The Air War in Indochina*, by the end of 1971 the US had dropped a total of

6.3 million tons of aerial munitions on the largely rural, agricultural Cambodia, Laos, and Vietnam, with the greatest
tonnage dropped between 1966 and 1968. An indication of the
massiveness of the air assault in Indochina was that during
World War II, in all its operations, the US dropped about two
million tons of munitions, while during the Korean War it
dropped about one million tons. Estimates of the number of
civilian casualties in the air war varied but were said to be in
the hundreds of thousands; the writers of *The Air War in
Indochina* said that during the intense phase of the bombing of
North Vietnam, there were "25,000 to 50,000 casualties per
year, 80 percent of whom were civilians. (An equivalent rate in
the U.S., given its greater population, would be 300,000 to
600,000 casualties per year.)"

A great deal of antiwar poetry and poetry by soldiers about
their combat experience was published in the late 1960s
and 1970s. Judging by what is reprinted in anthologies, almost
none of it of it is currently read. The little that does get reprinted
for new generations of students, however, is at least representative of the general tenor of antiwar poetry. Denise Levertov's
1971 "What They Were Like" imagines a person in the future,
a student perhaps, asking questions about the Vietnamese
culture before it was smashed by US bombs, and receiving
chilling answers. The question, for instance, of "Did they hold
ceremonies / to reverence the opening of buds?" is answered
with "Perhaps they gathered once to delight in blossom / but
after the children were killed / there were no more buds."
Robert Bly's 1967 "Counting Small-Boned Bodies" has a ghoul-
ish speaker doing enemy body counts – often fraudulent
body counts were used by the government to prove that
American forces were winning the war – and wishing that a
body could be shrunken down enough to fit into a finger ring
as a "keepsake." Bly's 1970 long poem "The Teeth Mother
Naked at Last" is an astonishing surrealistic account of

innocent Vietnamese peasants and their children dying grue-
some deaths at the hands of American soldiers and pilots. The
cause, Bly wrote, had deep roots in the American psyche and
American culture: the emptiness of American souls; the insan-
ity of trying to build democracy by killing people; the lies that
are spoken by ministers and priests, professors and newsmen,
as well as by the President; the affluence of the country as a
whole. Obviously, Bly was not trying to make a logical cause-
and-effect argument. His point was that the US was a madhouse and that the Vietnam War was a psychotic outbreak, a
construction of madmen politicians and generals in which
crazed, confused angry young men – juvenile delinquents
armed with the most lethal military hardware, so to speak –
were authorized to act out their violent propensities.

Bly's understanding of what Vietnam meant was not
unusual. It was similar to the vision in Norman Mailer's novel
Why Are We In Vietnam? (1967), to Mailer's vision of the
murderous, police-dominated America in *The Armies of the
Night* (1968), to Michael Herr's sense of Vietnam's hallucina-
tory qualities in his *Dispatches* (1977), and to the surreal
atmospheres which suffused many Vietnam combat novels and
films such as *The Deer Hunter* (1978) and *Apocalypse Now*
(1979). The Vietnam War, from these perspectives, was not a
foreign policy aberration, a strategic mistake, or a result of the
containment theory gone awry (George Kennan, incidentally,
was a war opponent). It was a manifestation of America's
madness and badness.

4

Places

The Context

Pride of place and ideas about the values associated with particular places always played important roles in American cultural history. Most individuals at least partly defined themselves by their origins, by the places where they were born. Given that Americans moved far more often than people in other countries, they also defined themselves by the places to which they migrated. Mass migrations, like the westward migrations of the 1930s and the black migrations to the North through much of the first half of the twentieth century, were in the American grain in the sense that economically driven migration had always been an important demographic element in US history. Getting on the road to new possibilities somewhere out there was an important element of cultural expression, as in some 1950s literature.

Very little housing construction took place during the Great Depression or World War II. At the end of the war, as soldiers returned, their housing needs were met by an extraordinary construction boom that helped to drive the great economic expansion of the late 1940s and 1950s.

The great majority of single family houses constructed during the postwar building boom were located in new suburbs. Some suburbs developed on the edges of large cities, some were small developments built on the edges of small towns located within about 20 miles of cities, some were built on vacant land within small cities located a few miles from larger cities, some were vast developments constructed on relatively remote farmlands. The most famous of the latter – which were sometimes said to symbolize the American future – were the Levittowns of William J. Levitt. The first Levittown was constructed in the late 1940s near Hempstead, Long Island. Using teams of workers and mass production techniques developed in the automobile industry, Levitt produced 17,000 houses. Each was set on a 60 by 100 foot (18 × 30 m.) lot. Each had four and a half rooms including a living room, two bedrooms and one bathroom. The least expensive sold for $7,900. Veterans could purchase one with a very small down payment and low mortgage interest rates. Later Levittowns in southern New Jersey and Bucks County, Pennsylvania, offered larger rooms and somewhat more stylistic variety.

The population of American suburbs grew by 46 percent in the 1950s. Over the next several decades, there was continued suburban growth, and by 2000 the country was often described as a "suburban nation."

A standard critique of suburban life developed among American intellectuals in the 1950s. The critique rarely mentioned that many blue-collar workers were drawn to the suburbs because of jobs – the number of industrial jobs in suburbs grew by 61 percent between 1948 and 1963. Nor did it take seriously the fact that many suburbanites, both blue collar and white collar, described themselves as pursuing their own understanding of the good life in a single family house with some healthful open space, friends and neighbors like themselves, neighborhoods and schools without juvenile delinquents, and so forth. Instead, the standard critique spoke of suburbanites as snobs, conformists, and empty people living meaningless lives. Later, in books such as Betty Friedan's *The Feminine Mystique* (1962), the loneliness and desperation of housewives confined in the suburbs became an element of the critique. By the mid-1960s, the critique also usually included the assertion that suburbanites were racists who had fled from city-bound blacks, that "white flight" was the root cause of suburbanization.

The standard critique had earlier intellectual roots. In a 1921 essay titled "The Wilderness of Suburbia," the architectural historian and critic Lewis Mumford had written that "The [suburban] man is a man without a city – in short a barbarian. Small wonder that bath-tubs and heating systems and similar apparatus play such a large part in his conception of the good life. These are the compensations that carry him through his perpetual neurosis."[1] In some ways, Mumford's statement repeated earlier biases in favor of the city and merely sub-stituted "suburbanite" for "country bumpkin" or "hick." Forty years later, Mumford became even more vitriolic, describing Levittowns as oppressively standardized and

> inhabited by people of the same class, the same incomes, the same age group, witnessing the same television performances, eating the same tasteless prefabricated foods, from the same freezers, conforming in every outward and inward respect to a common mold manufactured in the same central metropolis. Thus the ulti-mate effect in our time is, ironically, a low-grade uniform environ-ment from which escape is impossible.[2]

Another critic, John Keats, was also often quoted as an authority. In his *The Crack in the Picture Window* (1957), Keats wrote that

> For literally nothing down ... you too can find a box of your own in one of the fresh-air slums we're building around the edges of American cities ... inhabited by people whose age, income, number of children, problems, habits, conversations, dress, possessions, and perhaps even blood type are also precisely like yours. ... [The suburbs] are developments conceived in error, nurtured by greed, corroding everything they touch.[3]

A few years after Keats made his comments, the songwriter Malvina Reynolds wrote "Little Boxes," a bright, funny description of cookie-

[1] Lewis Mumford, "The Wilderness of Suburbia," *New Republic*, 28 (September 7, 1921), pp. 44–5.
[2] Lewis Mumford, *The City in History: Its Origins, its Transformations, and its Prospects* (Harcourt, Brace, and World, New York, 1961), p. 486.
[3] John Keats, *The Crack in the Picture Window* (Houghton Mifflin, New York, 1957), pp. xi-xii.

cutter suburban houses inhabited by the same doctors, lawyers, and business executives who all had the same children.

The standard critique of suburban life was developed in movies such as *No Down Payment* (1957), which stressed suburban alcoholism and racism, and *Rebel Without a Cause* (1955), which stressed the emptiness of suburban family life. Suburban emptiness was a major theme in a number of later movies including *The Graduate* (1967), *The Swimmer* (1968), *Ordinary People* (1980), *Edward Scissorhands* (1990), *Serial Mom* (1994), and *American Beauty* (1999).

The most influential account of suburban conformism was William H. Whyte's *The Organization Man* (1956). Based partly on Whyte's research in suburban Park Forest, Illinois, and on his experience as a business writer and editor for *Fortune* magazine, the book argued that bureaucratized modern corporations sought and rewarded only those employees who were *not* innovative, who were *not* individualistic. In a chapter titled "The Tests of Conformity," Whyte reported on the use of personality tests by corporate employers, and he made two ironic suggestions to job applicants. The first was, "When asked for word associations or comments about the world, give the most conventional, run-of-the-mill, pedestrian answer possible." The second was to remember during tests that "I loved my father and mother, but my father a little bit more; I like things pretty much the way they are; I never worry about anything; I don't care for books or movies much; I love my wife and children; I don't let them get in the way of company work."[4]

It was rare for defenses of suburban life to be published. The most famous literary defender was Phyllis McGinley, a mid-century poet and essayist. In "Suburbia, Of Thee I Sing!" McGinley argued that condemning suburbia had long been a "literary cliché":

> I have yet to read a book in which the suburban life was pictured as the good life or the commuter as a sympathetic figure. He is nearly as much a stock character as the old stage Irishman: the

[4] William H. Whyte, *The Organization Man* (Simon and Schuster, New York, 1956), pp. 196–8.

man who "spends his life riding to and from his wife," the eternal Babbitt who knows all about Buicks and nothing about Picasso, whose sanctuary is the club locker room, whose ideas spring ready-made from the illiberal newspapers. His wife plays politics at the P.T.A. and keeps up with the Joneses. Or – if the scene is more gilded and less respectable – the commuter is the high-powered advertising executive with a station wagon and an eye for the ladies, his wife a restless baggage given to too many cocktails in the afternoon.[5]

In place of the clichés, McGinley offered a picture of her Westchester County, NY, community that stressed its diversity, its civility, and its small town values and outlooks.

Some mid-century sociologists argued that suburban communities were far more complex and interesting than critics allowed. Pioneering studies of American suburban life included William Mann Dobriner's *The Suburban Community* (1958), Bennett Berger's *Working-Class Suburb* (1960), and Herbert Gans's *The Levittowners: How People Live and Politic in Suburbia* (1967). Gans's book provided a clear account of the various reasons people gave for moving to suburbs, including the desire for small-town life. Another study by Gans, *The Urban Villagers* (1962), suggested that ethnic neighborhoods in big cities actually functioned as villages or small towns, and that big cities were actually sequences of contiguous small towns.

While postwar suburbanization was taking place, many Northeast and Midwest cities that had been the country's major manufacturing centers began to steadily lose population. In fact, over the period from 1950 to 2010, while the country as a whole was growing from a 1950 population of 150 million to an estimated 2010 population of 308 million, many of those cities – Baltimore, Boston, Buffalo, Chicago, Cleveland, Detroit, Milwaukee, Minneapolis, Newark, Philadelphia, Pittsburgh, and St Louis – steadily declined, in some cases losing more than one-third of their 1950 population base. New

[5] Phyllis McGinley, "Suburbia, Of Thee I Sing!" *Harper's*, December 1949, pp. 78–82.

York City declined from 7.9 million in 1950 to 7.0 million in 1980, then began a steady increase to its projected 2010 population of 8.4 million. Since 1990, rates of decline in some cities have slowed, and Chicago and Minneapolis have experienced small increases of population.

Population declines translated into lost tax revenues for local governments and, consequently, declines in city services, education, job opportunities, and real estate values. Poverty rates and housing abandonment increased. The decline of real estate values and the increase in abandonment was exacerbated as real estate appraisers and banks "redlined" some neighborhoods, that is, outlined in red ink on city maps those neighborhoods judged to be full of bad risks and deteriorating housing. Disinvestment in city neighborhoods and investment in suburban development had for many years been a by-product of Federal Housing Administration policies that favored low-risk loans for new dwellings in new, homogeneous middle-class communities.

Not all cities declined. Many warm-climate "sunbelt" western, southwestern, and southeastern cities grew between 1950 and 2010, mostly as a result of migrations of people from the Northeast and Midwest. To many observers, though, sunbelt cities were not actually cities in the old sense but entirely new kinds of places, that is, sprawling suburbs and small cities within larger cities.

Black migration out of the southern states, steady for much of the twentieth century, accelerated in the 1940s, when 1.6 million left, and in the 1950s, when 1.5 million left. In that same period of time, in the South and in other sections, blacks became increasingly concentrated in segregated central city neighborhoods. By the late 1960s, the 12 largest cities – New York, Chicago, Los Angeles, Philadelphia, Detroit, Baltimore, Houston, Cleveland, Washington, St. Louis, Milwaukee, and San Francisco – contained more than two-thirds of the black population outside of the South and one-third of the total black population of the US. Washington was two-thirds black by 1968, many others were more than 30 percent black. In short, at the same time that white people (and jobs and money) were moving from cities to suburbs, black people were moving into the largest cities, most of which, because the loss of white populations outpaced the gain of black populations, were entering a long period of decline. Some readers might ask at this point why black people didn't also move to the suburbs. The answer to that is simple. With the exception of suburbs contiguous to cities and historically black suburban communities, the American suburbs were segregated, and blacks were not welcome. In some instances, the segregation was by law, but even as civil rights legislation was being passed and major Supreme Court decisions declaring segregation to be unconstitutional were being issued, the *de facto* segregation of places of residence continued throughout the country.

Earlier, the miserable circumstances, frustration, and anger of ghettoized black people had been dramatically and accurately described in the work of Richard Wright, Langston Hughes, Ralph Ellison, Gwendolyn Brooks, Ann Petry, Amiri Baraka, James Baldwin, and many other black writers. In his 1963 book *The Fire Next Time*, Baldwin dismissed the idea that the 1954 Supreme Court decision outlawing segregation had changed things for black Americans or represented a change of heart by whites, saying that most blacks he knew understood that recent concessions were motivated by the need for the US to seem progressive, especially to decolonizing Africans, in order to better fight the Cold War. Baldwin's point was that blacks could not be mollified by words and court rulings, and he predicted that before long there would be eruptions of black anger.

He was right. Between 1965 and 1967, several hundred disturbances occurred each summer in black areas of cities (the entire period was sometimes called "The Long Hot Summer"). The largest of them – the riot in the Watts area of Los Angeles in 1965, the Newark, NJ, riot of 1967, and the riot in Detroit, which began less than two weeks after the Newark riot – involved great numbers of participants, a tremendous amount of property damage, and many injuries and deaths. Local police were sometimes not capable of restoring order and, in fact, sometimes created more disorder by their presence and behavior. Militarizations occurred, usually by National Guard troops but in the case of Detroit by the insertion of 4,700 elite 82nd and 101st Division troops.

After the Detroit riot, President Johnson appointed a study commission, known as *The National Advisory Commission on Civil Disorders*, which investigated, heard testimony, consulted experts, and issued a 600-page analysis in 1968. The Commission did not mince too many words, arguing, for instance, that the frustration and anger of so many black people was caused by white racism, that city police departments treated black people unjustly and often brutally, that city education systems performed poorly, that black men and women lacked job opportunities, and that the country was becoming two separate and unequal societies. The report usually managed to translate its thoroughgoing, sophisticated analyses of sociological and economic data into prose that could be understood by common readers. Its recommendations for action were sensible, though in most instances politically impossible. There was even a candid "Conclusion," a half-page comment inserted before the "Supplement and Appendices," which recognized that the Commission had

> uncovered no startling truths, no unique insights, no simple solutions. The destruction and the bitterness of racial disorder, the harsh polemics of black revolt and white repression have been seen and heard before in this country. It is time now to end the destruction and the violence, not only in the streets of the ghetto but in the lives of the people.[6]

According to the Commission, the three most commonly cited grievances of ghettoized black Americans had to do with police practices, unemployment and underemployment, and housing. It was clear throughout the Commission analysis that, objectively and empirically, the grievances about housing were legitimate. The Housing Act of 1949 had established as a national goal, the Commission said, "the realization of 'a decent home and suitable environment for every American family.'" That lofty goal was

---

[6] US Riot Commission, *Report of the National Advisory Commission on Civil Disorders* (U.S. Government Printing Office, Washington, DC, 1968), p. 483.

obviously being accomplished in suburban America and in the parts of cities inhabited by white people, but it was not being achieved or even worked towards in black areas. In a devastating statement, the Commission summarized its findings:

> Fifty-six percent of the country's non-white families live in central cities today, and of these, nearly two-thirds live in neighborhoods marked by substandard housing and general urban blight. For these citizens, condemned by segregation and poverty to live in the decaying slums of our central cities, the goal of a decent home and a suitable environment is as far distant as ever.[7]

What was meant by substandard housing was housing that was old, deteriorating or dilapidated, and overcrowded.

By the later 1960s, a significant number of influential social commentators believed that cities were becoming places inhabited only by poor black people while suburbs were largely populated by mindless, conformist, racist whites. This unrelentingly pessimistic description of American places was depressing enough. To it was added the even more pessimistic description by environmentalists of the large-scale, long-lasting, and potentially apocalyptic misuse and destruction of the natural environment by humankind and, more particularly, by American corporations. The fundamental premise of environmental science was that the natural world was a vast, multilayered, multidimensional, delicate whole comprised of parts which existed in fragile relationships to one another and to the whole. This natural environment could be damaged when even a tiny part was destroyed; when enough parts were destroyed, the whole could crumble. The picture of the threatened natural world was first brought to large postwar reading audiences in books such as marine biologist Rachel Carson's *The Sea Around Us* (1951), *The Edge of the Sea* (1955), and *Silent Spring* (1962) and anthropologist Loren Eiseley's *The Immense Journey* (1957).

---

[7] US Riot Commission, 1968, p. 467.

Over the ensuing decades, in scientific reports and popular accounts, there developed a broad understanding of widespread environmental and ecological damage caused by smokestack industries, automobiles, pesticides, and chemicals. As a result of public health investigations, there also developed a broad understanding of the dangers of such commonly consumed items as tobacco, processed foods, and fast foods. All of those understandings developed amid worldwide concerns about natural resource depletion, the arms race between the US and the Soviet Union that had already spewed huge amounts of radioactive poisons into the atmosphere and that could ultimately end in nuclear holocaust, and actual disasters and near-disasters such as the March 1978 partial core meltdown of a nuclear reactor at Three Mile Island in Pennsylvania, the April 1986 explosion of a nuclear reactor at Chernobyl in the Ukraine of the Soviet Union, and the December 1984 gas leak at a Union Carbide pesticide factory in Bhopal, India.

Revulsion was a primary response to the developing understanding of declining cities, suburban "emptiness," runaway technologies, and impending environmental doom. Especially in the 1960s and 1970s, this revulsion was often expressed in "back-to-earth" social movements. While varying in their particular approaches, many groups called for the development of humane technologies and of loving relationships between individuals and the environment and the recognition of the primacy of community well-being as opposed to corporate profits. Many promoted dietary purity through organic foods.

Hundreds of rural communes were established in the 1960s and thereafter. Communes were often the subject of magazine and newspaper articles and were sometimes subjected to serious social science field study, as in Hugh Gardner's *The Children of Prosperity: Thirteen Modern American Communes* (1978). The "back-to-earth" movement as a whole was widely discussed in alternative periodicals like the Berkeley *Barb*, the East Village *Other*, the Milwaukee *Kaleidoscope* and in the most famous counterculture publication of the day, the *Whole Earth Catalog*. The fall 1968 *Catalog* briefly (but not so clearly) summarized the movement goals:

We *are* as gods and might as well get good at it. So far, remotely done power and glory – as via government, big business, formal education, church – has succeeded to the point where gross defects obscure actual gains. In response to this dilemma and to these gains a realm of intimate, personal power is developing – power of the individual to conduct his own education, find his own inspiration, shape his own environment, and share his adventure with whoever is interested. Tools that aid this process are sought and promoted by the *Whole Earth Catalog*.

The Literature

In chapter 3, I discussed some writing focused on the experiences of ghettoized black populations. Here, I will first comment on some writing about southern places, then on writing about suburban places, then on the literature of open spaces. Places obviously do not exist as entities separated from human culture. In particular, places are associated with forms of work (or lack of work, as in deindustrializing midcentury cities). Consequently, my discussions involve work issues as they are expressed in the literature of the early postwar suburbs and in Norman Maclean's *A River Runs Through It and Other Stories*.

In a 1954 talk that was later published as "Place in Fiction," the Mississippi writer Eudora Welty remarked that "fiction depends for its life on place," that the feelings of fictional characters are "bound up" in place. In a great deal of southern and other regional literature that represented stable rural cultures, place was a metaphor for local values that continued across time; to reside in a place was to reside in and to be shaped by a set of associations, values, beliefs, ways of speaking, weather conditions, landscape features, and so forth. The interconnection of place and human character had prevailed since "man stopped wandering," according to Welty. Displaced people and rootless people, this seemed to imply, were therefore lacking important elements that made for continuity and stability. Indicating how these concepts functioned in literature, Welty remarked that William Faulkner, "the triumphant example in America today of the mastery of place in fiction," wrote with "marvelous imaginative power" and also with the "carefullest and purest representation"; his "Spotted Horses," for example, was the "most thorough and faithful picture of a Mississippi crossroads hamlet that you could ever hope to see." At the end of her talk, she expanded that idea by saying that "the art that speaks most clearly, explicitly, directly and passionately from its place of origin will remain the longest understood." Such art, Welty said, was sometimes condescendingly called "regional" by "outsiders."[8]

Flannery O'Connor said in a 1963 talk titled "The Regional Writer" that the best American fiction had always been regional and that the "ascendancy" of regional fiction had "passed roughly from New England to the Midwest to the South; it has passed to and stayed longest wherever there has been a shared past, a sense of alikeness, and the possibility of reading a small history in a universal light." O'Connor was skeptical about the ability of outsiders to interpret the regional literature of the south: "For no matter how favorable all the critics in New York City may be, they are an unreliable lot, as incapable as the day they were born of interpreting Southern literature to the world."[9]

O'Connor's fiction, which she said she wrote as a Roman Catholic writer confronting the Protestant South, often dealt with such issues as religious belief, sin, and redemption and almost always invited readers to uncover and to debate embedded religious meanings. The standard O'Connor stories – the ones most often anthologized have been "A Good Man is Hard to Find," Good Country People," and "The Life You Save May Be Your Own" – typically include representations of simple southern country people whose self-awareness and understanding of the world around them is minimal and who speak in clichés, truisms, and platitudes, and representations of religious fanatics and seekers who often arrive unannounced at the homes of

---

[8] Eudora Welty's "Place in Fiction" is available at http://nbu.bg/webs/amb/american/5/welty/place.htm
[9] Flannery O'Connor, "The Regional Writer," in *Collected Works* (Library of America, 1988), pp. 847, 845.

the simple folk. Conversations among O'Connor's characters are often disjointed, full of non sequiturs, often seemingly pointless, and redundant. Endings are often violent as in "A Good Man is Hard to Find," or humbling as in "Good Country People," or full of strange prayer and deliverance as in "The Life You Save May Be Your Own" where a cloud "shaped like a turnip," following a "guffawing peal of thunder," rains raindrops "like tin-can tops" on the car of the constantly seeking Mr. Shiftlet.

Read without reference to their religious themes, O'Connor's stories seem to depict southern country people mostly as cartoonish hayseeds and ignoramuses. Read with reference to their religious themes, they seem to depict southern country people as cartoonish hayseeds and ignoramuses who sometimes have weird religious predilections. Both types of reading reinforce old cultural stereotypes of southerners and of the backward life of the countryside. A similar reinforcement of the old stereotypes was involved in James Dickey's characterizations of his backwoods men in *Deliverance* (1970) which, like O'Connor's stories, was set in Georgia.

Toni Morrison's *Sula* (1973), which has usually been read as a novel about the relationship of two young women, also contains some interesting perceptions about the culture of a black community in rural Ohio. The neighborhood called the Bottom in Medallion, Ohio, is in some respects as stable and unchanging a place as any small community written about by Faulkner, Welty, or O'Connor. Morrison's hamlet is almost completely isolated from the nearby white community, has little connection to other parts of the country, and so lives completely within itself, developing its own culture, its own tough-minded and innovative ways of enduring, its own ways of coping with the world and, in the chief conflicts of the novel, with local people who are different. There are, of course, variations among individuals, especially among the women who are its central characters. Ultimately, the Bottom, which began its life in the late nineteenth century, is overtaken by suburbanization as white Medallion moves outward. In the final chapter of *Sula*, titled "1965," Morrison writes that "the Bottom had been a real place" and that "Now there weren't any places left, just separate houses with separate televisions and separate telephones and less and less dropping by."

As could be expected, because the United States became an increasingly suburban country, suburbia (and "exurbia," the outer edges of suburbia) became the characteristic setting of American fiction in the second half of the twentieth century and in the early twenty-first century. Distinguished work such as John Updike's four "Rabbit" novels, telling the life story of one character in Pennsylvania, as well as his stories set in a Boston suburb, provides a complex representation of middle-class life. Richard Ford's "Frank Bascombe" trilogy was a brilliant extended account of southern New Jersey suburban life; *The Lay of the Land* (2006) is as detailed and sharp a representation of the suburban landscape as has been written. A considerable amount of Philip Roth's fiction, while often remembering childhood and young manhood in Newark, NJ, is suburban. Gish Jen's *Mona in the Promised Land* (1996) depicts life in a Chinese family in suburban Scarsdale in Westchester County, NY. In his novel *A Free Life* (2007), Ha Jin follows a Chinese immigrant from his American beginnings in Boston, to Manhattan, and then to suburban Atlanta, where he operates a Chinese restaurant. I will return to Jen and Ha Jin, as well as Roth, in the next chapter.

The most widely read literary works engaged with suburban life just after World War II, at the beginning of suburbanization, were John Cheever's Shady Hill short stories, Sloan Wilson's *The Man in the Gray Flannel Suit* (1955), and Richard Yates's *Revolutionary Road* (1961), from which a 2008 film was made. Each was set in the Westchester County or southern Connecticut suburbs of New York City. Cheever's affluent Shady Hill was a fictional version of Ossining, NY, one of the northernmost of the suburbs arrayed along the Hudson River, where Cheever lived for many years; the setting for Wilson's novel was about 30 miles away, in southern Connecticut; Yates's novel was set near the border of Westchester and Connecticut. There were working-class suburban communities in the general area – including some diverse but segregated working-class populations in the small Westchester cities of Yonkers, White Plains, and Mount Vernon – but they were in no way visible in the fiction.

Like a great deal of nonfiction commentary of the period, and like
other fictions, the characters in Cheever, Wilson, and Yates suffer
from similar problems. They have bad memories of the war; in
Cheever stories these memories are stated quickly, while in Wilson
the memories of Tom Rath are always near the surface. Young people
get married for poor reasons. In marriage, women lose whatever
identities they may once have had; after a few years, their husbands
begin having extramarital affairs. In many instances, children are
neglected. Money and social status, especially as symbolized by the
family house, are main motivators, and the loss of status is a constant
threat. In Wilson and Yates, characters believe that moving to a different place will resolve their current problems. Heavy drinking is
constant. What the men work at, how they do their jobs, what their
jobs *mean* aside from a paycheck, is their constant worry and, sometimes, their constant shame.

What people work at is barely mentioned in Cheever's Shady Hill
stories. A job loss, though, is a disaster. In "The Swimmer," we learn
that the main character, who is apparently undergoing a complete
"nervous breakdown," has recently lost his job and, after that, his
home and family. In "The Housebreaker of Shady Hill," the main
character is driven to steal money from his neighbors because he has
left his old job and is failing at his new job as an independent busi-
nessman working out of a small office. The work that Tom Rath does
in *The Man in the Gray Flannel Suit* and that Frank Wheeler does in
Revolutionary Road is a prominent part of their lives but, according
to them, is totally stupid, redundant, and meaningless.

Tom spends his days writing and rewriting a short speech on
mental health for his boss, the workaholic head of the United
Broadcasting Company. He struggles until he recognizes that, at age
33, he is faced with spending the rest of his life commuting to his job
in New York, reading annual reports, and "writing endless letters"
for his boss. Near the end of the novel, he describes his experience
after he came back from the war and saw:

a lot of bright young men in gray flannel suits rushing around New
York in a frantic parade to nowhere. They seemed to me to be

pursuing neither ideals nor happiness – they were pursuing a routine. For a long while I thought I was on the side lines watching that parade, and it was quite a shock to glance down and see that I too was wearing a gray flannel suit.

That brief description became iconic in the 1950s: the man in the gray flannel suit became the prime metaphor of the period to describe the conformist young. Tom, though, escaped the common fate in the novel, for, supported by his forgiving and endlessly decent wife, he decides to take another path (which is where the novel ends).

Frank Wheeler of *Revolutionary Road* faces different problems in his work life than Tom Rath faces and overcomes. Frank works in an ugly cubicle at Knox Business Machines, an old company going into the new computer business in the mid-1950s. His cubicle-mate is an alcoholic older man whose 10-year career at Knox had "been distinguished by an almost flawless lack of work." Frank is following in his footsteps, having learning how to appear to be working but actually doing nothing whatsoever except moving the same papers to different positions on his desktop. Working, then, actually meant spending days gossiping with coworkers, drinking at lunch, looking at the young secretaries and receptionists, with one of whom Frank carries on an affair. Ironically, Frank finally does a little work, does it well, is discovered by the big boss, and is given a promotion. In this way, long-term work avoidance and malingering is not punished by the company but, in a twisted way, is rewarded. In the complications of the novel's plot, the promotion leads to his refusal to go along with his wife's plan to move to Paris, where she will work while Frank "finds himself," and ultimately to his wife's death as a result of her attempt to abort the baby she is carrying.

Educated, middle-class, white suburbanites (or urbanites, for that matter) who lack "meaningful" work and who therefore spend their time malingering on the job became stock cultural figures and fairly common fictional figures after their postwar beginnings in Cheever, Wilson, and Yates. Obviously, they sharply contrast with characters in fiction by contemporary black writers such as Ellison, Petry,

Baldwin, Baraka, Brooks, and Morrison (whose characters in *Sula* are often denied decent employment).

One of the constants of nineteenth- and earlier twentieth-century American cultural history was the idea of leaving the overdeveloped, corrupted, unnatural world behind and establishing a new, free, unconstrained life "out there" in open, sparsely settled landscapes. That idea fired the imaginations of pioneers, readers of boys' adventure stories, and advertising copywriters for companies and railroads selling uncultivated land at low prices. In one form or another, it was a major theme in classic nineteenth-century writing such as James Fenimore Cooper's Leatherstocking novels, Henry David Thoreau's *Walden*, and Twain's *Huckleberry Finn*. It recurred, as I indicated earlier, in twentieth-century writing such as Cather's *O, Pioneers!* and *The Professor's House* and Fitzgerald's *The Great Gatsby*.

The attraction of open landscapes – the love of the vistas available in large horizontal spaces – often involved a concomitant revulsion against cities and other places where men and women gathered to conduct the workaday business of the world. So it is not surprising that a body of fairly recent American literature features the open spaces, the unspoiled towns of the hinterlands, the threatened but still intact natural environment. In Kerouac's *On the Road* there are frequent appreciations of the lay of the land and of looming mountains. Nabokov's *Lolita* includes a tour of some of the country's back roads. The two books are interesting reflections of the postwar popularity of automobile tourism in the country (including the summer 1953 cross-country car trip of former President Truman and his wife). William Least Heat-Moon's *Blue Highways: A Journey into America* (1982), the author's record of his long trip through localities beyond the superhighways and fast-food joints, is in that same tradition. The popular anthology *The Norton Book of Nature Writing* includes work by novelists and poets Wallace Stegner, Maxine Kumin, Gary Snyder, Wendell Berry, N. Scott Momaday, Jim Harrison, William Least Heat-Moon, Maxine Hong Kingston, Alice Walker, Annie Dillard, Barry Lopez, Gretel Ehrlich, Leslie Marmon Silko, Jamaica Kincaid, and Louise Erdrich. Many of them grapple with the psychological effects of space on human beings; many revel in the fact that what seemed lost in congested places was preserved in faraway landscapes.

In *About This Life* (1998), Barry Lopez argued that landscape "feeds us, figuratively and literally" and that memory "protects us from lies and tyranny." "To keep landscapes intact and the memory of them, our history, in them, alive," Lopez summarized, "seems as imperative a task in modern time as finding the extent to which individual expression can be accommodated, before it threatens to destroy the fabric of society."[10] Lopez's comments on preserving and remembering places that shape us could stand as a summary of the fundamental points of a great deal of writing about the natural environment. In a 1985 essay titled "The Solace of Open Spaces," Gretel Ehrlich conveyed the feel and texture of life in the endless spaces of Wyoming, the silences and solitudes and the loss of "the distinction between background and foreground" and remarked that "people here still feel pride because they live in such a harsh place, part of the glamorous cowboy past. ..."[11] Ehrlich's remarks about the mentalities produced by openness summarize a fundamental perception of the literature of open spaces. I understand that both Lopez and Ehrlich may sound very abstract and disconnected from context to readers who have been taught to think of the Wyomings of the subcontinent as lying in "the middle of nowhere."

The most popular literary work concerned with landscape memory published in recent decades was Norman Maclean's *A River Runs Through It and Other Stories* (1976). What is remembered in it is the open, near-pristine early twentieth-century Montana landscape, especially the Big Blackfoot River. How it is remembered varies. On the one hand, Maclean conveys a geological understanding of the landscape, writing about it at some length in the language of the earth sciences. On the other hand, he writes about it as a sacred

[10] Barry Lopez, *About This Life: Journeys on the Threshold of Memory* (Alfred A. Knopf, New York, 1998), p. 143.
[11] Gretel Ehrlich, "The Solace of Open Spaces," in *The Solace of Open Spaces* (Viking, New York, 1985), p. 3.

religious place full of magic and beauty, a place where God is manifested as at the beginning of time. Some of the descriptions in the
book are as "painterly" as any produced by an American writer. But
throughout, whatever the perspective on it, landscape is also deeply
entangled with memories of family relationships.

Maclean's title story involves a good deal of fly fishing for the
enormous rainbow trout of the Blackfoot, and so many of its nature
descriptions involve landscapes framed by unfolding fly lines. The
younger brother in the story, Paul, is a master with a fly rod, an
"artist." One of many descriptions of him is done in an Impressionist
style that emphasizes light and change:

> Below him was the multitudinous river, and, where the rock
> had parted it around him, big-grained vapor arose. The mini-
> molecules of water left in the wake of his line made momentary
> loops of gossamer, disappearing so rapidly in the rising big-grained
> vapor that they had to be retained in memory to be visualized as
> loops. The spray emanating from him was finer-grained still and
> enclosed him in a halo of himself. The halo of himself was always
> there and always disappearing, as if he were candlelight flickering
> about three inches from himself. The images of himself and his line
> kept disappearing into the rising vapors of the river, which continu-
> ally circled to the tops of the cliff where, after becoming a wreath
> in the wind, they became rays of the sun.

For this particular scene – which is one of several performances by
Paul set against the backdrop of the pristine landscape – there are
two other spectators in addition to the narrator: a "motherly" woman
in bib overalls who is awed into a simple "My, my" by Paul's performance art and her equally awed husband who keeps on repeating
"Jesus" as he looks (a tease for some readers because of the fish sym-
bolism in Christianity, because of Paul's "halo," and because we have
just been told that Paul is 32 and "at the height of his power").

In the story, Paul works as a reporter on a Helena, Montana,
paper. But he does that work only because it gives him time and
money to pursue his real vocation as a great "artist" fly fisherman.
However, it should be added that Paul is a heavy drinker and gambler,

which makes his story an interesting new version of the old story of the gifted artist who is simultaneously an undisciplined, self-destructive fool.

Some readers have been drawn to *A River Runs Through It and Other Stories* because of its landscape elements. Some have been attracted by its fishing elements; it can be read as a virtual instructional manual on streamside ethics, on the basics of how to use a fly rod, on how to get the big ones, on how Paul Maclean has moved beyond the ordinary rhythms of fly casting, taught to him by his father, to create rhythms of his own. Those readers and others, I believe, were also drawn to it because of Maclean's expression of socially conservative family values (the term "family values" is itself associated with modern American conservatism) and his very traditional view of manhood or manliness. In some respects, Maclean's views on male roles echo those in classic American writing by Robert Frost and Ernest Hemingway and they comport with views often expressed in union and other working-class writing. As in Frost, they have a conservative dimension.

Most interesting to me, Maclean argues for the power and "art" of male work and the bonding strength and power of all-male work cultures. This is a conscious element in the book. On one occasion, he told an audience that he had written "love stories: stories of my love of craft – of what men and women can do with their hands." On another such occasion, he said that the book rested on

> three closely related aspirations: (1) to depict the art and grace of what men and women can do with their hands in the region of the country that I was brought up in and know best; (2) to impart with a description of these arts something of the feeling that accompanies their performance or, indeed, of intelligently watching them performed; and (3) of seeing in the parts of nature where they were performed something like the beauty, structure, rhythm, and design of the arts themselves.[12]

---

[12] Norman Maclean, "The Hidden Art of a Good Story: Wallace Stegner Lecture," in Ron McFarland and Hugh Nichols (eds), *Norman Maclean* (Confluence Press, Lewiston, ID, 1988), p. 29

"USFS 1919: The Ranger, the Cook, and a Hole in the Sky," the third of the three stories that make up *A River Runs Through It*, tells the story of Norman Maclean's summer work at age 17 with the tough guys who worked in the United States Forest Service in its earliest years. At the center of Norman's work gang are two "artists." Bill Bell is a ranger who is also the head packer of horses for hazardous trips through the Idaho wilderness. Packing, Maclean says, "is an art as old as the first time man moved and had an animal to help him carry his belongings," and Bill Bell was a "major artist" capable of producing a "masterpiece in that now almost lost art" by perfectly balancing a string of nearly 50 horses. The camp cook, who is much despised by Norman, is a card shark. Bill tells Norman that the cook is not just a card shark but is an "artist," and Norman then says that he understood that in "the center circle of male magic sits the card shark, but Bill's calling him an artist was something I wouldn't accept." The point is made, though, that Norman will not punch the cook, as he would love to do, no matter what.

Within this world headed by artists is a gang of hard, uncomplaining men who do their work and who at the end of the summer bond together when they go to town to whore, to gamble, and to get into an explosive bar fight that Maclean details with great care and obvious pleasure. There are scapegoat men, too, the sorts of negative role models who seem always to exist as scapegoats in all-male work cultures. Some of the workers hired by the Forest Service in the hiring halls of Butte and Spokane were "bums off the street, miners out of the holes for the summer with the hope of avoiding tuberculosis, winos, and Industrial Workers of the World." The worst of these, the laziest, the most untrustworthy, the ones that would spread fires so they could stay on the government payroll were the IWWs, the "I Won't Works," Maclean says, repeating the old nickname used by the capitalist opponents of the IWW and setting himself apart from the great number of American writers and academics who have lionized and romanticized the IWW since the earliest years of the twentieth century. Working-class solidarity obviously has its limits. The work gang is for serious workers, artists, and artists-in-training like young Norman, not for fools and malingerers.

"Logging and Pimping," the second of the stories, takes place in an Idaho logging camp in the summer of 1927, when Norman is home from graduate school in the East (he later became a professor of English specializing in Shakespeare at the University of Chicago). It tells of working on two-man crosscut saws, "things of beauty," with Jim, the fiercest fighter, best womanizer, and best logger around. He is as tough as they come (I have not counted but "tough" is used dozens of times to describe these men), a Jack Dempsey-like big man feared by other big men, even by the camp cook, the "guy with the golden testicles," as the workers describe him. At one point Maclean remarks that "The world of the woods and the working stiff was pretty much made up of three things – working, fighting, dames – and the complete lumberjack had to be handy at all of them" (I will remark here that that also pretty much sums up the world of my own youthful summers working construction and factory jobs in the wide open spaces of the Bronx in New York).

"Logging and Pimping" turns partly on fear and foreboding about Jim. He tries to wear Norman out on the two-man saw – "maybe what he had been doing this summer was giving me his version of graduate school," we are told – but he does not succeed and thereby becomes Norman's best pal. It also turns partly on Jim's sexual prowess, including his doings with a good-looking rancher's wife who rides into camp Sunday after Sunday with a bucket to gather huckleberries, is guided by Jim into the woods, and returns through the camp, to the great appreciation of the other loggers, without any huckleberries and without her bucket. Finally, it turns partly on Jim's contradictions. He is scornful of his fellow workers' complaints about the company and he calls them "incompetent sons of bitches," but he is a socialist who spends his winters reading socialist literature at a Carnegie library in town, where he also pimps a whore, an unsocialist vocation if ever there was one. The story ends with the socialist sawyer cum pimp writing a one-line letter to Norman that sums up some of his craziness and crudity in the sort of stark language that men use with their best pals: "Just to let you know I have screwed a dame that weighs 300 lbs."

In Maclean's title story, Paul is judged by his toughness and his artistry. In the two other stories, men are judged primarily by their skills as workers, with some possessing skills so highly developed that they are artists. Near the end of "USFS 1919" Maclean says:

> we were a pretty good crew and we did what we had to do and we loved the woods without thinking we owned them, and each of us liked to do at least one thing especially well – liked to swing a jack-hammer and feel the earth overpowered by dynamite, liked to fight, liked to heal the injuries of horses, liked to handle groceries and tools and tie knots. And nearly all of us liked to work. When you think about it, that's a lot to say about a bunch of men.

What needs to be added here is that Maclean, narrating these stories, shows how much he loves to describe the *processes* by which work gets done. There are long passages describing in elaborate detail things like sawing a log, what type of clothes and boots are best in the woods, how to set up a prostitute to do business, how to balance loads on pack horses, doing smoke-watching from the tops of mountains, cutting trail, fighting forest fires, playing cards, preparing for the bonding ritual of "cleaning out the town," coordinating the punch-out. This is fiction about enthusiastic, joyful work, about labor done with care and verve, about manly tasks most of which have long since been lost, about skills of another time and place. I can think of no other post-1945 literature that is analogous to it. Of earlier writing, I can think of no other works that have similar outlooks except some Robert Frost poems and Ayn Rand's *The Fountainhead*.

Maclean was no doubt aware that there would be readers who would not believe that fly fishing was an "art" rather than a game or sport or that the other artists in the book were anything more than crude men. That is probably why he laid into the title story a scene that describes the tattoo on the buttocks of a local prostitute. Paul Maclean observes that she "has LO tattooed on one cheek of her ass and VE on the other." Norman says, "LOVE spells love, with a hash-mark between." I may be guilty of pushing things too far here, but I think that what Maclean has in mind is the most frequently seen art image of the 1970s, Robert Indiana's "LOVE," reproduced 320 million times by the US Post Office as a stamp in 1973 and placed as a sculpture in many municipal parks. If that is art, Maclean seems to ask, why can't fly fishing or tying knots or sawing logs be art, too?

"Progressive" ideology of the 1960s and 1970s, at least as translated in the mass media, typically claimed that brutish men who cannot communicate were the source of vast social dysfunction, that men needed to become more "feminine" and more in touch with their inner selves, that cultural diversity needed to be valued, and so forth. It was deeply hostile to the increasingly Republican, conservative politics and work cultures of male construction/building trade workers and other skilled manual workers, and, as the period developed, there were increasing signs of deepening hostility on the part of such workers to antiwar and civil rights activists, feminists, defenders of the idea of reproductive privacy rights, and the Democratic Party. Caricatures of dumb, racist, brutish, sexually predatory, oppressive male workers allied to the Republican Party abounded in academic and other elite media.

As I understand it, *A River Runs Through It and Other Stories* is a conservative response to the "progressive" conventional wisdom of the time. The book's conservatism – here I mean its *social* conservatism – involves several of the core contemporary issues: the roles of women and men, the degree to which men should be self-defining and self-reliant, and attitudes toward outsiders. Maclean argues very clearly that the roles of women and men are separate and distinct, that men must be as self-reliant as possible and must maintain a stoic silence in the face of pain, and that outsiders should be treated with distrust and hostility (the world, according to the young Paul, "was full of bastards, the number increasing rapidly the farther one gets from Missoula, Montana"). In the later 1960s and 1970s there was a "rediscovery" of traditional women's arts and crafts, including needle crafts, quilting, weaving, and doll making. Much of the emphasis in academic feminist studies, as well as in popularizations of these expressive forms, was on community building and the power of female traditions, especially in rural communities. Maclean does not reject those ideas. But, despite his statement about his wish to "depict the art and grace of what men and women can do with their hands" in his region of the country, he says nothing about any woman's art or craft. Instead, his family-oriented women, as opposed to the whores in the book, are depicted in traditional roles only, cleaning fish, cooking, waiting patiently for their men, and so forth. He is completely absorbed with the power and art of male work and the bonding strength and power of all-male work cultures. His outlook is wholly traditional and nostalgic.

The 1992 Robert Redford film of *A River Runs Through It* – which has had many times more viewers than the popular book has had readers – is similarly nostalgic and traditional. It makes its points, though, in different ways. It hardly touches on the action of the two shorter stories and it plays down most of the technical elements of fly fishing (actually, the fly fishing that occurs in the movie is fairly stiff and constricted, lacking the power and grace that Maclean wrote about). In the voiceover at the beginning, it is announced that the film is about to tell the "classic story of an American family" set in a "land untouched" and in its opening minutes it provides extended treatment of the cute preteen Maclean brothers, Norman and Paul, whom the book treats in five pages. It moves all the important adult action of the title story back from 1937 to 1926 and thereby, among other things, substitutes the narrator's pretty courtship of Jessie for their developed and sometimes difficult marital relationship. It invents scenes of church-going and grace-saying, community dances, family conferences, Norman's home schooling, a community picnic, a network of friends of the Maclean brothers, a double date by the brothers which takes place in a picturesque vintage speakeasy, and a visit by the brothers to a brothel-cum-gambling house that Paul frequents. It also invents whole scenes on the river, such as a wild boat ride by the Maclean brothers down whitewater chutes and over a substantial waterfall, as well as a scene in which Norman's Jessie takes him on a harrowing shortcut by driving down railroad tracks, through a tunnel, and over a narrow trestle. It has Norman at Dartmouth College as a student, teaching Romantic poetry to freshmen while also teaching his fraternity brothers how to play poker as it is played on Front Street in Missoula, and at the end of the movie taking a job at the University of Chicago as an instructor of English literature (the letter flashed on the screen also says that he has been admitted to the graduate program). Some of this material was imported by Redford from interviews with Maclean and lectures by him in the years after he published his book. Some was pure creation for the film.

The film *A River Runs Through It* explores and endorses traditional rural values, the grandeur of the still unspoiled American landscape of the early twentieth century, and family values (while not neglecting family dysfunction and tragedy). The conservatism and nostalgia of the film is not a distortion of the book so much as it is an elaboration of it for a mass movie audience.

5

Immigrant Destinies

Old Immigrants

The context

Beginning in 1917 and culminating in the 1929 National Origins Quota Act, the US government passed a number of laws sharply curtailing mass immigration. Under the terms of the 1929 Act, the annual ceiling for immigration from northern and western Europe was set at 127,000 and the annual ceiling for immigration from southern and eastern Europe was set at 21,000 (in later years, there were some modifications of those numbers); Asian immigration was completely banned. Immigration from Western Hemisphere countries such as Canada and Mexico was not restricted under the terms of these immigration laws.

There were some signs of change in immigration policy during and just after World War II. Trying to undergird its wartime alliance with China, the government repealed the Chinese Exclusion Act in 1943. Beginning to use immigration policy as an instrument of foreign policy and potential geopolitical advantage over the Soviet Union, the government in 1946 gave Filipinos naturalization rights and began to permit immigration from India (in later years, there were significant numbers of political refugees permitted entry from Cuba, Southeast Asia, Eastern Europe, and elsewhere). But postwar liberalization in some areas of immigration policy was more than balanced by new restrictive laws. Some of these were outgrowths of the politics of anti-Communism. The 1940 Smith Act had authorized refusing visas to Communists and also permitted the deportation of alien Communists; the 1950 Internal Security Act provided that aliens who had been Communists or who had belonged to Communist front organizations in their home countries be barred from entering the country or deported if they had somehow already entered. The major postwar immigration legislation, on the other hand – the 1952 McCarran–Walter Act – endorsed national origins quotas, though it did provide 185 annual visas for Japanese, 100 for Chinese, and another 100 for people from other Asian-Pacific countries.

Images of Nazi concentration camps and stories of the suffering and deaths that had taken place in them were published soon after their liberation by allied forces. Immediately after the end of World War II, there were reports in the American and world press that millions of Jews had died in what would later be called the Holocaust.[1] Through 1946 and 1947, Nazi brutality was revealed in the Nuremberg Trials of German war criminals (the Tokyo trials of Japanese war criminals took place simultaneously).

There was considerable sympathy in the US for the surviving Jewish victims of the Holocaust and the destinies of other people displaced by the war in Europe. A number of American politicians, like their European counterparts, pressed for the opening of Palestine to Jewish refugees. Allowing some refugees, including Jews, into the US was discussed in Congress but no legislation resulted. In December 1945, understanding that it was unlikely that Congress would soon act, President Truman issued an Executive Order, which did not require Congressional approval, to expedite the admission of 3,900 refugees, or "Displaced Persons" each month.[2] The figure of 3,900, as the President was careful to explain, was exactly the limit set by the immigration quotas, so the order represented more a symbolic gesture than a policy change. Many Congressional Republicans and southern Democrats nonetheless continued to resist opening the country to refugees, arguing that it was a bad precedent that would

[1] See e.g., "80% of Reich Jews Murdered by Nazis," *New York Times*, June 10, 1945, p. 13.
[2] "President Orders Speedy Admission of More Refugees," *New York Times*, December 23, 1945, p. 1.

lead to a flood of Asian refugees; a *New York Times* editorial singled out the resistance of the Chair of the Senate Immigration Committee, Richard B. Russell (Democrat, Georgia), in discussing the relatively small effort that the country was being called to make on behalf of displaced persons.[3] Indicating the grassroots strength of the resistance, two months later the American Legion, the organization which represented veterans of the two world wars, declared its opposition to admitting refugees because they would "increase the distress" of unemployed veterans by competing for jobs.[4] In 1948, Congressional and grassroots resistance to the immigration of displaced persons eased somewhat and the Displaced Persons Act was passed, permitting about 200,000 visas to be issued. By 1952, under the terms of the Act and its amendments, it was estimated that about 80,000 Jewish DPs had settled in the US.

In November 1947, the newly formed United Nations, recognizing the need for a Jewish homeland, voted to partition Palestine. Palestinian leaders rejected the partitioning of their country, of course, which led to a civil war between Jews and Arabs in 1947 and 1948, and finally to Israel's declaration of independence and statehood. The US was the first country to recognize Israel and since 1948 has regarded Israel as its most reliable ally in the troubled, oil-rich Middle East, supporting it through several wars with its neighbors while pursuing and brokering an endless number of peace initiatives. In recent decades, even fundamentalist American Christians have become staunch supporters of Israel in the hope that a large and final Arab–Israeli war would fulfill biblical predictions of the end of the world and the Second Coming of Christ.

Traditional American anti-Semitism has continued apace despite American support of Israel. Old ideas of Jewish control of the international banking system and Jews as "Christ-killers," murderers of Christian children, and so forth, have continued to circulate.

[3] "The 'DP's Are No Menace," *New York Times*, September 4, 1946, p. 7.
[4] "Legion Will Fight Admission of DPs," *New York Times*, November 1, 1946, p. 17.

"Holocaust denial," the idea that the Nazi murders did not happen, has become a staple of ultra-right discussions in the US, as in Europe. The futuristic novel *The Turner Diaries* (1978), by the white suprema-cist leader William Luther Pierce III under the pseudonym Andrew Macdonald, was the most recent "literary" expression of anti-Semitism (as well as the expression of murderous rage about black people and immigrants). As told by Macdonald, the liberation of white gentiles from Jewish tyranny begins when Congress passes the "Cohen Act," which outlaws all private ownership of guns. This was the final straw in what had been the long worldwide domination of Jews, a domination that resulted from the weakness of whites: "If the white nations of the world had not allowed themselves to become subject to the Jew, to Jewish ideas, to the Jewish spirit, this war would not be necessary," the narrator says at one point while at another he expresses his rage at Jews as the cause for "the decomposition of races and civilizations." Near the end of *The Turner Diaries*, there is nuclear war that leads to the incineration of Jewish centers such as New York City and Israel.

The Turner Diaries, which was sometimes distributed free at gun shows and ultra-right gatherings but also sold several hundred thou-sand copies, did not live simply as a novel. The main perpetrator of the 1995 bombing of the Oklahoma City Federal Building that resulted in 168 deaths and 680 injuries had a copy of *The Turner Diaries* with him when he was arrested. The bombing itself was modeled on the bombing of FBI headquarters in Washington, DC that the novel said was one of the first acts of the white revolution.

No other American ethnic group rooted in the nineteenth century or in the twentieth century before the quota acts drew anything like the attention that Jews drew in the decades after World War II. But old stereotypes of other ethnic minorities persisted in American popular culture, of course. Irishmen still drank heavily and were prone to violence. Italians were still Mafiosos and/or crude, overfed dumbbells, as in a never-ending stream of movies and television series from *The Godfather* through *Goodfellas*, *The Sopranos*, and the current (in 2010) *Jersey Shore*. Polish people were still dumb. And so forth. P. J. O'Rourke's 1976 parody of the stereotypes captured a considerable part of the extreme hatreds involved.[5] Jews were alone, though, in being perceived as so powerful, so victimized by world events, so important to American foreign policy, so crucial to maintaining access to oil, or, in the eyes of ultra-rightists and their allies, so destructive.

The literature

In Bernard Malamud's *The Assistant* (1957) and his collection of short stories, *The Magic Barrel* (1960), prewar and postwar Jewish refugee characters have nothing to do with large global issues and have no power whatsoever. Stories such as "The First Seven Years," "The Mourners," "Angel Levine," "Take Pity," and "The Loan," like *The Assistant*, depict refugees struggling to make a living in rundown or marginal New York neighborhoods. Business is never good and there are few chances for a better life except, possibly, for the Americanized children. Poverty and despair are not Malamud's primary subjects, however. Rather, the subjects are how to care for others despite the struggles of one's own life, how to love, how to retain the Jewish cultural traditions despite living in an alien place, despite the recent history of Jews in Europe, and sometimes despite flawed personal histories. Jews, though, are not the only people who keep the faith of human connection. There are good Italians in Malamud's neighborhoods, as in the stories "The Prison," "A Summer Reading," and "The Bill," and as in the character Frank Alpine in *The Assistant*.

Not all Malamud characters remain moral Jews. A number resist the needs of others and take no pity on people who have less than themselves. Some absorb the individualist, materialist values of the mainstream culture. Henry Levin in "The Lady of the Lake" changes his name to Henry R. Freeman, "had often been in love," seeks love in Italy, finds it (or at least finds someone who is physically

---

[5]   O'Rourke, "Foreigners Around the World," was published in *National Lampoon* in May, 1976 and is available at http://www.olimu.com/notes/Foreigners/Foreigners. htm.

beautiful), denies his Jewishness in order to get her, and is ironically rejected by her because she is a Jew who has survived a concentration camp and will only accept a Jewish man as her husband. The rabbinical student Leo Finkle in "The Magic Barrel" seeks a wife through a matchmaker, rejects women as potential mates based on their physical appearances or age, and ends up falling in love with the picture of one girl who, ironically, is described by her father, the matchmaker, as a "wild one" who is "without shame" and who he considers to be dead. The completely self-absorbed Finkle, believing that marriage should be based on "love," insists on meeting the girl. A meeting is arranged by the matchmaker, and the daughter appears as a mid-twentieth-century stereotype prostitute, standing under a streetlight smoking a cigarette while her father "chanted prayers for the dead." How far Finkle has absorbed American ways and stale popular culture imagery is indicated when Malamud says that Finkle sees in the girl's eyes "desperate innocence" (a phrase that sums up the popular image of the prostitute as hurt child), sees in her "his own redemption" (summing up the popular notion that a man can be saved by a woman), and when, in a flourish that could have been plagiarized from any number of Hollywood boy-meets-girl films, Malamud says that "Violins and lit candles revolved in the sky. Leo ran forward with flowers outthrust."

The notion that Jews are all the same is repudiated by the work of a great number of prominent post-World War II Jewish writers and public intellectuals such as Arthur Miller, J. D. Salinger, Norman Mailer, Saul Bellow, Allen Ginsberg, Philip Roth, Joseph Heller, E. A. Doctorow, Erica Jong, Vivian Gornick, Cynthia Ozick, Betty Friedan, Paul Goodman, and Bob Dylan. Among those writers, Philip Roth has been the most consistently absorbed with questions of Jewish identity and history and with the cultural tensions within Jewish communities. "Defender of the Faith," an early Roth story that has often been anthologized, represents a number of tensions having to do with Jews serving in World War II and others utilizing their Jewishness as a way to avoid service. The title novella of *Goodbye, Columbus* (1960), a collection of stories that included "Defender of the Faith," was set against the backdrop of the sharp cultural differences between Jews who remained in Newark, New Jersey, the city of Roth's childhood, and upwardly mobile Jews who had moved to wealthy suburbs and joined country clubs. The novel *Portnoy's Complaint* (1969) became a landmark in the history of Jewish-American writing because of its exploration of subjects that no other Jewish writer explored so thoroughly (or so outrageously). In later novels such as *American Pastoral* (1997), *I Married a Communist* (1998), and *The Plot Against America* (2004), Roth deepened and sharpened his representations of Jewish life in the mid-century US.

Alexander Portnoy of *Portnoy's Complaint* is a stereotypical studious Jewish boy who becomes the Assistant Commissioner of Human Opportunity in New York, a position which sounds perfect for a caring Jewish man who wishes to lift up the downtrodden. His parents are caring and giving, solicitous of Alexander's needs, and intent on raising him properly. The father lived for his family: "In that ferocious and self-annihilating way in which so many Jewish men of his generation served their families, my father served my mother, my sister Hannah, but particularly me." The mother, who could have stepped from the pages of Dan Greenburg's 1964 comic *How To Be A Jewish Mother*, attempted through guilt and fear to totally control her son's behavior; she is, according to Portnoy, an "unforgettable" woman "who could accomplish anything, who herself had to admit that it might even be that she was actually too good."

A Jewish upbringing was in theory supposed to produce children who honored their parents with unbounded filial piety. What is produced in Alexander Portnoy, though, is shockingly, perversely the exact opposite of what the theory claims. The memory of the father as "self-annihilating" ultimately ends with Portnoy calling him "this schmuck, this moron, this Philistine father of mine." The memory of the mother as "too good" continues in considerable detail before it ends with Portnoy asking his psychiatrist to say why his mother pointed a knife at him when he was seven because he would not eat some string beans and a potato and why his father did not stop her. Those questions are of course not answered but lead directly into the notorious second chapter of *Portnoy's Complaint*, which describes in hilariously graphic detail how Alexander spent his adolescence masturbating, sometimes with the aid of unusual devices (a milk bottle, a piece of liver, a cored apple). He explains his obsessive masturbation to the psychiatrist – like other mid-century "bad boy" fictions, a psychiatrist is the addressee in *Portnoy* – as the inevitable result of his mother's power and dominance: his penis, he says, was "all I really had that I could call my own." At the end of the chapter, he asks the psychiatrist to save him, to "Bless me with manhood! Make me brave! Make me strong! Make me *whole*! Enough being a nice Jewish boy, publicly pleasing my parents while privately pulling my putz! Enough!" In short, Jewish parenting of the kind that he has experienced leads to Alexander's infantilization, to his later avoidance of Jewish women as partners, to his voracious appetite for sex, and still later to sexual dysfunction when he finally desires a Jewish woman, who happens, in an especially appropriate comic twist, to be a soldier in the Israeli army.

Voracious sexual appetites are not unusual in youth-running-wild literature and Roth's Portnoy is not unlike, for example, the speaker in Ginsburg's *Howl*, Kerouac's Neal Cassady, Mailer's hipsters, Tom Wolfe's Ken Kesey, and some of Charles Bukowski's more extreme characters. But he alone is tortured and he alone traces his problems to his parents or indeed sees them as problems and not as signs of revolutionary consciousness. Jewish mothers and fathers, we are invited to believe, make even their most rebellious sons into candidates for extended psychotherapy – the breaker of stereotypes is stereotypically guilt-ridden.

In much of his most recent work, Roth has been essentially historical in his approach to ongoing Jewish issues. *American Pastoral*, set in the late 1960s and early 1970s, remembers the first- and second-generation Jews who helped to establish Newark as a major manufacturing center. The glove factory owned by the Levov family on which the novel is focused employs highly skilled craftsman who take great pride in their work; families in Jewish Newark are close; there is a shared sense of community. That old world is now crumbling on several fronts. After the Newark riots of the 1960s, there are business declines and "white flight." At the national level, there is Vietnam and Watergate. Families and individuals are weakened by the excesses of the "sexual revolution." Within the family of Swede Levov, which has moved to a beautiful farm in an idyllic rural landscape 30 miles away from Newark, a child becomes an antiwar bomber and a close associate of ultra-left ideologues, leaving her parents searching for meaning and psychological stability. *I Married a Communist*, published a year after *American Pastoral*, focuses on the impacts of post-World War II anti-Communism on some Jews in Newark, brilliantly portraying the psychological damage that individuals suffered. Like *American Pastoral*, the novel indicates Roth's disgust with how the US evolved in recent decades. Among left-liberal writers, Jewish as well as non-Jewish, disgust was not an unusual response to the sharp rightward thrust of American culture that had roots in the 1930s and 1940s and accelerated after 1980 or so.

The Plot Against America imagines the 1940 election of aeronautical pioneer and culture hero Charles Lindbergh to the American presidency, the Nazi-friendly foreign policy that is put into place by the Lindbergh administration (in real life, Lindbergh was isolationist and sympathetic to Germany), and the repressions against Jews that quickly evolve. As in *American Pastoral*, the Jewish community of Newark is pictured by Roth as assimilated, content in its Americanness. The child who narrates the story says at the outset that his family had had "a homeland for three generations" and that he "pledged allegiance to the flag of our homeland every morning at school. I sang of its marvels with my classmates at assembly programs. I eagerly observed its national holidays, and without giving a second thought to my affinity for the Fourth of July fireworks or the Thanksgiving turkey or the Decoration Day doubleheader. Our homeland was America." Later, he says his American childhood was "incomparable." This enthusiastic love of country is balanced by a total proud absorption in Jewishness and a love of neighborhood.

The most self-consciously historical of Roth's work, *The Plot Against America* even includes a detailed postscript that indicates Roth's impressive understanding of the biographies of the major political figures woven into the novel and a good bibliography of some of the relevant scholarship on isolationism and prewar politics.

The postscript, Roth wrote, was "intended as a reference for readers interested in tracking where historical fact ends and historical imagining begins." Like the novel itself, it raises interesting questions about how engaged writing works and how it informs audiences who know from the outset that the imagined seminal event – the alignment of the US with Nazi Germany – did not happen.

The Plot Against America was published in 2004, a couple of years after the September 11 attacks and the beginning of what the American liberal-left commonly viewed as the repressive behavior of the Bush administrations (torture, imprisonment policies, the Patriot Act, the targeting of Arab-Americans, surveillance, assertions of unlimited Executive power, and so forth). It seems to invite readers to believe that Roth meant it as a commentary on the further move rightward that the country made after 9/11. But he addressed this issue in an essay titled "The Story Behind 'The Plot Against America,'" saying:

> Some readers are going to want to take this book as a roman a clef to the present moment in America. That would be a mistake. I set out to do exactly what I've done: reconstruct the years 1940-1942 as they might have been if Lindbergh, instead of Roosevelt, had been elected President in the 1940 election. I am not pretending to be interested in those two years – I *am* interested in those two years.

That statement is very clear. But, later in the essay, after recounting the critical moments he lived through as an American born in 1933, and remarking that "History claims everybody, whether they know it or not and whether they like it or not," Roth wrote about the provisional lives that people live, the surprises and shocks of events:

> And now Aristophanes, who surely must be God, has given us George W. Bush, a man unfit to run a hardware store let alone a nation like this one, and who has merely reaffirmed for me the maxim that informed the writing of all these books and that makes our lives as Americans as precarious as anyone else's: all the

assurances are provisional, even here in a 200-year-old democracy. We are ambushed, even as free Americans in a powerful
republic armed to the teeth, by the unpredictability that is history.[6]

The New Immigration

The context

Liberalism was triumphant during the Kennedy and Johnson
Administrations of the 1960s. Major legislation such as the Civil
Rights Act of 1964 and the Voting Rights Act of 1965 was aimed at
abolishing racial discrimination. The Hart–Celler Act of 1965 was
aimed at abolishing the ethnic discrimination codified in the national
origins quota system. Hart–Celler did away with the national origins
rules and established annual immigration ceilings: 170,000 visas were
allocated for people from the Eastern Hemisphere and 120,000 for
people from the Western Hemisphere. In 1978, the Act was amended
to remove the hemisphere allocations and a worldwide annual
admissions ceiling was set at 290,000. The immediate relatives
(parents, spouses, and children) of US citizens were exempt from the
worldwide limitation.

Immigration to the US dramatically increased in the decades after
1965. The 2000 Census indicated that 31 million people living in the
country, or about 10 percent of the population, were foreign-born.
If the children of the foreign-born were included in the count,
according to the Census, the "new American" population was 60
million, or 20 percent of the total. An indication of immigrant
youthfulness, and of how continuing and deep the impact of immigration on American culture was likely to be, was that 21 percent of
the country's under-25 population was foreign-born.

The US, it needs to be added at this point, is not in any way unique
in regard to contemporary immigration. Migration is a worldwide

---

[6] *New York Times*, September 19, 2004, p. C10; available at http://www.nytimes.
com/2004/09/19/books/review/19ROTHL.html

dynamic – in 2010, about 200 million people worldwide are living in countries in which they were not born. Migration and immigration is transforming every major region of the world.

In terms of their countries of origin, the new American immigrants were very different from their early twentieth-century counterparts. According to the 2000 Census, 51.7 percent of them came from Latin America and 26.4 percent came from Asia, while only 15.8 percent came from Europe (2.8% were from Africa, 2.7% from Canada, and 0.5% from Oceania). In terms of their education levels, the new immigrants were also profoundly different from their earlier counterparts. While 38.2 percent of the over-25 foreign-born population had not completed high school, 5 percent held associate degrees, 13.7 percent held bachelor's degrees, and 10.3 percent held graduate or professional degrees. The relatively high education levels of some immigrants were reflected by employment patterns: 28.4 percent held jobs in management, professional, and related occupations. There were, largely as a result of educational achievements, great variations in immigrant family incomes. In 2000, the median income of the households of the foreign-born ranged from a low of $29,388 for Latin Americans to a high of $51,363 for Asians. The percentage of immigrant families below the government-defined poverty level for a family of four was 15.3, about the same as for native-born Americans.

As indicated by a 2002 Census Bureau survey of communities, new immigrant populations were unevenly distributed across the country. The states with the highest concentrations of the foreign-born were California (26.9% of its total population), New York (20.9%), New Jersey (18.9%), Florida (17.9%), and Hawaii (17.9%). Some cities had especially high concentrations of foreign-born people: 60.6 percent of the population of Miami, Florida, was foreign-born. Other densely immigrant cities were Santa Ana, California (48.4%), Los Angeles (41.3%), Anaheim, California (40.3%), San Francisco (36.7%), New York (36%), and Houston, Texas (28%). As was the case during the immigration wave at the turn of the twentieth century, large areas of the US were almost untouched by the new immigration; there were few immigrants in states such as Mississippi

(1.1% of the total population), West Virginia (1.2%), and Montana (1.6%).

In recent decades, increasing numbers of immigrants have settled in suburbs as opposed to cities. According to a 2001 Brookings Institute study of the 102 most populous metropolitan areas, 50 percent of Asians and 50 percent of Hispanics lived in suburbs in 2000, most of them in so-called "melting pot" metropolitan areas such as New York, Los Angeles, San Francisco, Miami, and Chicago.

A great deal more is known about post-1965 immigration than was known by contemporaries at the time of the immigration boom at the turn of the twentieth century. Information about the new immigration is not limited to the statistical detailing provided by the Census Bureau, the Bureau of Labor Statistics, and other federal agencies. A major source of information about life within American ethnic communities is available through the contemporary database *Ethnic NewsWatch*, which reprints and usually translates articles about current events, political and social attitudes, and immigration trends that have appeared in the country's extensive foreign language periodical press. Moreover, there have been a great number of academic studies of the new immigration.

Illegal immigration has been a major problem in the US since the 1940s. During World War II, the government began the Bracero Program, which admitted Mexican farm workers (i.e., *braceros*) on short-term contracts that guaranteed work and living arrangements. Predictably, given the poverty of Mexico to which they were expected to return at the end of their contracts, many *braceros* stayed in the US and thereby became illegal aliens. They and others of their compatriots who simply illegally crossed the Mexican–US border were aggressively pursued by the Immigration and Naturalization Service (INS); between 1950 and 1955, the INS arrested and deported some 3.8 million Mexicans.

The problem of illegal immigration did not end. Between 1965 and 1975, after the passage of Hart–Celler, the INS averaged about 500,000 arrests and deportations annually. By 1986, it was estimated that three to five million illegal aliens were living in the country. In 2009, according to a respected 2009 Pew Research Center study, the number of illegal immigrants had grown to 11.9 million (out of a total population of 300 million), 55 percent of whom were said to be Mexicans. The great majority of illegal immigrants, whether of Mexican or other national origins, worked at low-skilled jobs at pay rates significantly lower than legal workers and, of course, rarely if ever complained about their working conditions, hours of work, and low pay. In that regard, from the points of view of many employers, they were ideal employees. A recent study, Patrick Radden Keefe's *The Snakehead: An Epic Tale of the Chinatown Underworld and the American Dream* (2009) explores in great detail how Chinese illegal immigration operates and benefits smugglers, businesspeople, and even, arguably, the poor Chinese peasants who pay great sums of money, up to $30,000, for the privilege of being smuggled into the US (most pay off their debts to the smugglers with years of labor).

It is not clear how many illegal immigrants think of themselves as permanent residents of the US. Return migration of legal immigrants to their home countries is commonplace – between 1966 and 1993, according to the INS, about one-third of immigrants went home – and the same is probably true for illegal immigrants. But there is evidence that some illegal immigrants stay in the US for extended periods of time. An effort to control the problem by giving illegal immigrants the opportunity to become legal was undertaken in 1986 with the passage of the Immigration Reform and Control Act, which gave people who illegally resided in the US after January 1982 legal status. In 1990, under the terms of the Act, 800,000 illegals were made into legal immigrants; in 1991, 1.1 million were legalized.

There has been significant resistance to immigration based on attitudes and fears that are more or less the same as those which propelled the anti-immigration movements of the late nineteenth and early twentieth century. The long list of the allegedly negative effects of the new immigration have included claims that the foreigners could not be Americanized, that some were criminals, that they were destroying American traditions, that they were lowering wages, that they were taking jobs that should go to "real" Americans, that they were costing taxpayers great sums of money, that if current immigration trends continued white people would become a minority in their own country. Not on the list was any claim about immigrants and radical politics, very probably because American radical politics has essentially disappeared from American life. In recent decades there have been some efforts by the federal government to seal the Mexico–US border more decisively, some grassroots movements agitating for immigration reform, and some interest in having Congress revisit immigration policy as a whole.

Moreover, the isolation of recent immigrants from other groups, their existence within homogeneous immigrant subcultures, is not significantly different from the class-based or race-based subcultures in which the great majority of "native" Americans live. That is to say, American culture is tremendously diverse and tremendously segregated too.

I will add an aside here: while both social science and literary representations suggest the separateness of immigrant enclaves, one set of facts, the intermarriage of Asian women and white men, dramatically indicates significant cultural mixing. According to a Census 2000 supplemental survey, 14 percent of Chinese women, 32 percent of Filipino women, 33 percent of Japanese women, 28 percent of Korean women, and 8 percent of Vietnamese women were married to white men. Each of those figures is extremely high for interracial marriages. Various reasons have been offered for why so many intermarriages occur.

The literature

Like most literature professors, I am leery about discussing very contemporary writing, mainly because I am not sure that writing that is now seen as important will continue to be seen that way in the future. But as I thought about how to conclude this book, I became convinced that I was obliged to provide readers with some understanding of the new immigration, arguably the most important culture-changing phenomenon of our time, and with some brief comments on some of the well-regarded writing published recently by new immigrants. A lot of that writing is wonderfully unique and varied, presenting points of view and worlds of experience that readers like me have never before come across. Much of it also engages two basic questions, one regarding the initial experiences of immigrants with the larger American society and one regarding the causes of migration.

I currently teach an undergraduate seminar on the literature of recent immigration in which students read Bharati Mukherjee's *The Middleman and Other Stories* (1988), Gish Jen's *Mona in the Promised Land* (1996), Junot Diaz's *The Brief Wondrous Life of Oscar Wao* (2007), and Ha Jin's *A Good Fall* (2009) along with short work by Sandra Cisneros, Maxine Hong Kingston, Helena Maria Viramontes, Judith Ortiz Cofer, Gary Soto, and Chang-rae Lee. In the works on my list, one of the basic features of recent immigrant experience in the US is that, regardless of origin, most immigrants are represented as having little contact with people who are not of their own immigrant group. They are, so to speak, *in* the US but not *of* it. There are exceptions, as in Gish Jen's *Mona in the Promised Land* and her story "In the American Society," because the well-to-do Chinese family Jen writes about lives in the wealthy white suburb of Scarsdale, NY, and the daughters grow up fully assimilated (Mona even decides to become Jewish). But Mukherjee's Indians are almost exclusively in touch with other Indians, Diaz's Dominicans are with other Dominicans (though Oscar Wao lives part of his life in the company of science fiction heroes), and Ha Jin's Chinese are with other Chinese. There is nothing new about these representations of first-generation and sometimes second-generation isolation (*voluntary* isolation for the most part, I think).

The question of why people migrate to the US, which in much of the recent literature of immigration seems always to be the predicate for character and action, has been represented in various ways. In Mukherjee's frequently anthologized short story "A Wife's Story," one of those in *The Middleman and Other Stories*, the main character is in New York studying for a PhD and experiencing a modern life, a sharp contrast to the life she could expect to have as a woman in traditional India. She describes the women of her family, saying "My mother was beaten by her mother-in-law, my grandmother, when she registered for French lessons at the Alliance Française.

My grandmother, the eldest daughter of a rich zamindar, was illiterate." She also describes the privileged training she has received, saying that "My manners are exquisite, my feelings are delicate, my gestures refined, my moods undetectable." Her next sentence indicates that her training was of no use except as a kind of defense: "They have seen me through riots, uprootings, separation, my son's death." The dangers of life for educated people in Third World developing countries is also remarked on in Jen's *Mona in the Promised Land*, where we learn that the parents left revolutionary China because, as well-to-do people, they would have been killed or, if they were lucky, would have had their property confiscated and been "re-educated" to be peasants.

In Ha Jin's novel *A Free Life* (2007), the effects of the 1989 Tianamen Square massacre of demonstrating students by the Chinese People's Army can be felt (Ha Jin has described himself as having stayed in the US, where he was a student, because of Tianamen Square). In *A Good Fall*, though, the causes of migrations to the Flushing, NY, Chinatown are less political. In "The Beauty," there is a reference to "an old Taiwanese couple who planned to move to Flushing from Switzerland because they could find genuine Chinese food here." In the title story "A Good Fall," the born-in-America Cindy describes her parents' move by saying, "This is America, where it's never too late to turn over a new page. That's why my parents came here. My mom hated her ex-mother-in-law – that's my grandmother – and wanted to restart her life far away from the old woman."

In Mukherjee, Jen, and Ha Jin, violence, political repression, and the oppression women experience in traditional societies simply because they are women are the major causes of migration by Asians. Literature depicting Latin American migrants often describes similar causes for migration. Helena Maria Viramontes' brilliant and intense short story "The Cariboo Café" describes the horrendous violence experienced by a young woman and her child during the 1980s civil war in El Salvador, shows her and other migrants experiencing the dangerous lives of illegals in the US, describes her pain at the murder of her child, describes the ignorant prejudices of Americans, and ends with her being killed by police. In *The Brief Wondrous Life of*

Oscar Wao, Junot Diaz describes the Dominican Republic as a corrupt, impoverished, violent, machismo-maddened, sex-crazed, fated, dilapidated place ruled by tyrannical men who treat women with sadistic cruelty. Given the opportunity, some people, including Oscar Wao's mother, a victim of Dominican machismo and sadism, are desperate enough and courageous enough to migrate to the US.

The US does not shine forth as paradise in any of this writing. But, for the most part, it is represented as considerably more respectful of differences among its people, considerably less sexist than traditional societies, and, perhaps most importantly, considerably more tolerant of immigrant subcultures. I do not think, however, that any of these positive attributes are experienced by the masses of uneducated, low-skilled legal and illegal immigrants, the displaced peasants from China's still-impoverished countryside, the uneducated Mexicans, Latin Americans, Haitians, and Jamaicans who cannot find work in their own countries. For those poor people, the US is probably just a place where work might be found, where body and soul can be kept together.

Index

Berger, Bennett, *Working-Class
    Suburb* 98
Bernstein, Leonard, and anti-
    Communism 32
Berry, Wendell 110
Bhopal, Union Carbide gas leak
    103
Bird, Caroline 67
black Americans
    in cities 99–100
    and CPUSA 10, 12, 15–16, 27,
        42–3, 46–51
    and happy Negro myth 76–7
    and jazz 66, 69, 78
    and mental illness 77–8
    rural 21
    and segregation 100, 102
    and student radicalism 86–7,
        88–9
Black Panthers 87, 88–9
Black Power movement 86–7
Black Student Union 84
black studies courses 84
Blackboard Jungle (film) 60
blacklisting
    and anti-Communism 31, 33
    prohibition 7
The Bloody Brood (film) 60
Bly, Robert 90–1
    "Counting Small-Boned Bodies"
        92
    "The Teeth Mother Naked at
        Last" 92–3
bop music 66, 75–6, 77
Bracero Program 132
Brando, Marlon 60
Brooks, Gwendolyn 100, 110
    "The Last Quatrain of the Ballad
        of Emmett Till" 79
    "The Mother" 79
    "The Sundays of Satin-Legs
        Smith" 79

"We Real Cool" 79
Browder, Earl, *What Is
    Communism?* 9–13
Brown, H. Rap, *Die, Nigger, Die!*
    86–7
Brown, Lloyd L. 48
Brown, Sterling A. 21
Bukowski, Charles, *Post Office*
    79–80, 127
Bulosan, Carlos
    "Be American" 21
    "Homecoming" 21
Burroughs, William J. 74, 76
Bush, George W. 129
Byrnes, James 28

capitalism
    and Communist writers 15–16
    and CPUSA 10, 15, 27
    "golden age" 52–3
    see also Great Depression
Capote, Truman, *In Cold Blood*
    70
Capra, Frank 20
Carnegie Endowment for
    International Peace 34, 35
Carson, Rachel
    The Edge of the Sea 102
    The Sea Around Us 102
    Silent Spring 102
Cassady, Neal 76–7, 80, 127
Cather, Willa
    O, Pioneers! 110
    The Professor's House 110
Chambers, Whittaker 34
Chaplin, Charlie, and anti-
    Communism 32
Cheever, John
    "The Housebreaker of Shady
        Hill" 108
    Shady Hill stories 107–8
    "The Swimmer" 108